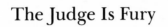

# The Judge Is Fury

# POETS ON POETRY · Donald Hall, General Editor

*Mary Kinzie*

# The Judge
# Is Fury

## DISLOCATION AND
## FORM IN POETRY

Ann Arbor
THE UNIVERSITY OF MICHIGAN PRESS

Published in the United States of America by
The University of Michigan Press
Manufactured in the United States of America
∞Printed on acid-free paper
1997   1996   1995   1994     4   3   2   1

*A CIP catalogue for this book is available from the British Library.*


Library of Congress Cataloging-in-Publication Data

Kinzie, Mary.
    The judge is fury: dislocation and form in poetry / Mary Kinzie.
        p.      cm.—(Poets on poetry)
    Includes bibliographical references.
    ISBN 0-472-09553-6 (alk. paper). — ISBN 0-472-06553-X
    (pbk.: alk. paper)
    1. Poetry—Book reviews.   I. Title.   II. Series.
PS3561.I59J8   1994
811'.5409—dc20                                              94-10261
                                                                CIP

# Acknowledgments

In the preparation of this volume and the essays that make it up, I should like to acknowledge the help, advice, and encouragement of Alfred Appel, Elizabeth Dipple, Donald Hall, Daryl Hine, Marjorie Perloff, Eleanor Wilner, and the editors who originally commissioned the articles. I would like to thank the poets whom I treat, many of them unknown to me, for their forbearance. The essays in this volume, all © by Mary Kinzie, originally appeared in the journals listed below, some in a different form. Grateful acknowledgment is made to these publishers:

"'How Could Fools Get Tired!' " *Poetry* (April 1978).

"The Music of Overemphasis" is taken from a longer review-essay called " 'What Are You Doing Up There in Those Grapes?' " *Parnassus: Poetry in Review* (Fall/Winter 1978–79).

"A Generation of Silver," *American Poetry Review* [hereafter *APR*] (July/August 1981).

"Biological Passion Play," The *Nation* (12 December 1981).

"Collected and Selected," *APR* (November/December 1981).

Review of *The Complete Poems of Marianne Moore*, Chicago Tribune *Book World* (26 July 1981).

"Native Voices," *Nation* (27 February 1982).

"Haunting," *APR* (September/October 1982).

"Rites of Understatement" is from "No Connection," *APR* (January/February 1983).

"Outsiders," *APR* (July/August 1983).

"Pictures from Borges," *APR* (November/December 1983).

"Among the Shades," *APR* (March/April 1984).

"Weeds in Tar," *APR* (July/August 1985).

"Thick and Thin," *APR* (November/December 1985).

"Lessons in Feeling: A Moral Essay" is from "Meaning in Place," *APR* (January/February 1992).

# Preface

What follows is a sampling of my work as a reviewer. A previous volume, *The Cure of Poetry*, collected general articles on poetry in an age of prose; the present volume is limited to the more ephemeral but in some ways more demanding form—the poetry review. From roughly six hundred pages of text not absorbed by the earlier book, and commentaries on one-hundred-some-odd poets, I have selected the essays and reviews that seemed to fulfill two criteria: I wanted the poet discussed to be good or bad in some interesting way; I also wished my treatment of the poems to be sharp and persuasive. In particular, in each I have tried to detect the collaboration of the unruly stranger who often writes alongside the poet, providing the necessary link to inspiration but at the same time threatening to derail the process of writing.

With these ends in view, I have left out of this collection work on a number of writers who might otherwise interest a literary audience—Sylvia Plath, Timothy Steele, and Richard Wilbur, for example—because it seemed to me I had not made much that was interesting out of my interest in them. Other writers (by far the greater number of those eliminated) I had not presented so as to make the flaws instructive.

What remain are the strongest and most representative discussions of the work of forty-five volumes of poetry from the articles and omnibus reviews I wrote between 1978 and 1992. For almost a decade, I was a staff reviewer for *American Poetry Review*. This meant that I read everything published in poetry in English the journal received for review. One difficulty faced by any reviewer sifting through such large numbers of books is that the work usually does not have time to settle in one's sensibility. It is rather hard to say what will prove lasting when one has only a month or two to try out a book's staying power.

But it soon became obvious that there was too little of even hypothetical merit on the poetry scene to warrant two or three long reviews each year, and consequently that I should have to devise some approach for treating the books I chose other than the criterion of obvious and continuing importance to literature. And yet I felt I had to maintain the ideal of the poet as someone who strives toward importance in much the way poets have always done—by engaging with the literature of the past and reaching through it to an individual aesthetic.

What I decided to do in these reviews was to explain why and how the little good poetry was good, and not to flinch from pointing out why and how the preponderating bad poetry was bad—in light of this idea that a writer must approach the craft and calling of poetry as a listener, and inheritor, first. But from the features that make bad poetry bad (which I am moderately confident I can make sense of) I have hesitated to derive a general prescription for what must in all times and places make poems good. The critic should always be able to recognize the presence of something passionately *other*, although there is no one way for this presence to make itself felt. Even poet-critics I very much admire—T. S. Eliot, for example, Randall Jarrell, and the prolific Howard Nemerov—are better when they refrain from the prescriptive impulse in order to look at the particular good. By and large it is just as difficult to move from the specific negative features of one example of badness to a general negative proscription. Even W. H. Auden, for all the liveliness of his pronouncements, is a case in point.

Auden has an arresting argument for the tenacity of kitsch in poetry of a high caliber—but it is an argument so subtly attuned to the artistic flaws in one writer especially as to seem a law for one. He offers as the most insidious of three possible avenues to badness in poetry (the first two being slipshod or careless work—*vide* Shakespeare on occasion—and oversights that lead to unintentional comedy) a third way: This is a "corruption of consciousness," which leads to "intentional badness. . . . [O]ne feels certain that the poet is very pleased with it." Trash, he points out, is the inevitable result whenever a person like Tennyson "tries to do for himself or others by the writing of poetry what can only be done in some other way, by action, or study, or prayer" (see the 1944 essay on Tennyson in Auden's *Forewords and Afterwords*, 1974).

When poets misunderstand the purpose and proper arena of poetry, making it do the work of some other endeavor, one often finds today a form of therapy whose goal is not discovery but confirmation. In the absence of genuine therapeutic possibility, however, the critical audience is implicitly neutralized. Therapeutic kitsch is designed, above all, to fend criticism off. And because the first thing a serious critic must do is to expose and dismantle the machinery of poor art and false feeling, there is inevitably a degree of rancor displayed by a certain class of professional amateur and self-therapist toward the commentator who takes the role of critic seriously. This resistance is one reason why so few writers want to be critics.

But this task is more thankless now than it might once have been. One reason is the obvious drop in literary culture since midcentury. Along with the fading of literary "literacy" comes the disturbing possibility that modernism has opened a Pandora's box of egalitarian cliché that cannot be closed again. It is the assumption of many writers that there is no going back to earlier forms and modes, even those that seemed so rich and capacious, so genial and effective in producing an illusion of civility and even grandeur. Nor can one keep on copying the disruptive homages of modernism. In fact (or so the future-sensitive attitude would seem to dictate), it would be culturally false and invariably a debasement of one's own period's authentic urges even to *attempt* to go back.

Whatever one's response to them, these views are epochal ones: Poetic possibility is seen as categorically different now than it was before Pound and Eliot. One group might suggest that the arts were reduced to the demotic, on the whole, at a certain point in time, and that there is no way to correct this regenerating, or perhaps accelerating, downward trend: One can only continue along one's way, ignoring it if possible. Then there is a second group, who, sharing this essentially deterministic view, decide not to regret the outcome—who, on the contrary, embrace the notion that whatever happens in culture is laudable.

The first view is articulated by F. T. Prince in a letter to John Ashbery in 1958, composed in equal parts of admiration and irritation at the American poet's personal unpredictability and his poetic habit of inclusiveness (Ashbery seemed to him to take up the second view, essentially receptive to many of those forms of popular culture that strike Prince as a debasement of high culture). "Why have you ever imagined," he asks, "that the movies, or popular music, or television or radio could ever be anything but rubbishy and futile?"[1] Prince admits he may be wrong, but values the gain in "simplification" which his admittedly intransigent (and dated) stuffiness affords him. But about one thing he believes he is correct:

> ... the 'modern movement' in everything, which began with heroic figures like Pound and Eliot, had in it from the beginning the seeds of the imbecile proliferation which we now suffer,—the organised racket of creative writing, action painting, etc. etc. There is no foreseeable end to this, it can only go on being more so, more itself, as long as the world lasts.

Prince, himself a splendid poet (his *Collected Poems* are discussed on pp. 47–54), is clearly a purist of style and a romantic in temperament whose peculiarly beautiful poems indicate a level of psychic struggle and controlled achievement not possible when the style radically (but intelligently) oscillates, as it does in Ashbery. On the other hand, few poets have Ashbery's energy in confronting over and over again the "imbecile proliferation" of the products of consciousness. Too many contemporary poets in the postmodern period can address the inevitable debasement of mental life in popular forms only by reproducing it. At the same time, Prince may be confusing cause with one effect of the disappearance of the poetic genres. In lieu of a rich vocabulary of discrimination between elegy and satire, epigram and lyric, there is no gauge by which to bar any material from any sort of poem.

The difficulty of criticism can thus be seen as one result of the experiments that have successively abraded the authority of literacy and the traditions of literary forms. F. T. Prince locates this fundamental revolt with modernism. Others go further back. A longer historical view is taken by the writer-philosopher Iris Murdoch. We inherit from the Enlightenment and Kant an idea of the individual as free, potent, and alone. To these notions clustering about the isolated will more recent cultural trends have added the corollaries that man is educable, that he can know himself through psychological analysis, and that his highest achievements are those of accurate and searching self-expression, or sincerity.[2] "We no longer see man against a background of values, of realities [social, national, religious], which transcend him." Instead of a "rich, receding background," ever seductively incomplete, says Murdoch, the world has been flattened by the ease and convenience of comprehending it empirically. Social and political complexity have been flattened, too. "What we require is a renewed sense of the difficulty and complexity of the moral life and the opacity of persons." Murdoch's call for eloquence is paradoxically one that demands of the artist truth-telling and acceptance of incompleteness rather than closure in the work of art, along with a renewed dubiety and complication in the moral and spiritual realms imaged there.

I am not sure which of the two epochal explanations is the more pertinent one. Both seem arguable. Surely we are equally post-Enlightenment, postromantic, and postmodern—with all the usual weaknesses and restrictions that come with diminished things. But we are also (despite Harold Bloom) potentially as liberated by apprenticing ourselves to the past as we are paralyzed by its finished gestures. *Contra* Auden, it seems to me that we benefit from insisting that poetry ought to do for ourselves and others what is imaged in other humanizing pursuits such as prayer, study, and action against affliction. I would agree with Murdoch that the more encompassing is the array of impulses subjected to aesthetic control, the greater will be the works that result. Consider Auden's own finest poems, among them "The Shield of Achilles," with its historical and ethical sweep, and "In Praise of Limestone," in which his love of geology and his religious beliefs come together, albeit sublimated by satire. It narrows poetry to assume that it may receive only those impulses that are not siphoned off into acts of intellect, argument, and devotion. At the highest level poetry taps every energy; it also refracts those energies and meditates about them by means that emerge during the poet's training. One anecdote will illustrate my sense of the liberation that counteracts any small-scale anxiety one might indulge toward the forerunners.

A man wakens in a desert with a continuous thong, like a Mobius strip, drawn so cleverly about his ankles that he can neither untie it nor walk upright. He stands, falls, stands, starts to hobble, falls, stands again. He does brief, birdlike leaps, one foot slightly behind the other. He becomes better at this. He drinks from muddy pools; he eats roots. Having nothing to do in this wasteland with its monotonous horizon, he becomes adept at long leaps upward, then forward; he practices coming down so as to raise only the lightest puff of dust from the friable earth. A whimsical interpolation to this allegory would have us believe that a circus travels past the man and seeing his graceful movements engages him to be its rope dancer high above the audience. What is beyond dispute is that the moment someone cut the thong it was as if the Achilles tendons had been severed and the man could neither dance nor walk. One version of this story, called "The Bound Man" ("Der Gefesselte"), is told by the Austrian writer Ilse Aichinger.

If it be asked whether one couldn't have learned to rope-dance anyway, the answer would have to be, How could one stop striding ahead for long enough to stumble back upon the alien measures of rope-dancing? To be an apprentice is to learn someone else's angle of vision till one is blind with it. Like writing with the wrong hand, learning art is at first as unnatural as any broken habit. Over time, this thwarting and unpleasant wrongness is absorbed and adjusted until it not only casts no shadow but even enables one's very seeing, dexterity, and repose.

Many apprentice poets have not yet begun to learn the stumbling that leads to a different level of progression. And since they have not yet begun to creep, let alone to dance, their recoil from the complex impediment of their own inheritance deceives them into thinking their broad, efficient pace is winsome. To them one might recall J. V. Cunningham's mordant quatrain with its unnerving clause casting all the neatly fitting poetic relationships into doubt:

> These the assizes: here the charge, denial,
> Proof and disproof: the poem is the trial.
> Experience is defendant, and the jury
> Peers of tradition, and the judge is fury.[3]

To begin with, there is the exercise of mature craft upon the pondered experience of one's life. Upon these themes and techniques the accumulated conscience of literate critics and readers balances and brings to bear judgments regulated by the history of the writing one is trying to do—these are the "peers of tradition" (Cunningham's jury, which weighs one's concerted skill).

But after the most stern and sympathetic scrutiny is applied, there is still the jealous, ravening judge of fury who throws us into despair. This force, categorically outside the poet's control, looms up from a deeper dimension like one of those libidinal energies that brings a civilization to life—and even after its provenance is recognized, the poet can only prepare against its coming as for an invader, while hoping (against hope) that it will indeed arrive. Above all, grace does not descend upon the artist who wants it easy. Nor does grace always make smooth. The peculiar semantic lurches and circular querying of Wallace Stevens's greatest poems indicate the high toll taken by idiosyncrasy. The muse comes only when one can face her companions, death, oblivion, and the incapacity represented by such companionship, and continue, in some fashion, to work.

The present age is not (if any age was ever) propitious for poetry; oddly, it is even less so for criticism. But then, mercifully, from time to time, when there is some conversation with the past, some familiarity with forms, some breadth of human interests, and some flexible familiarity with fury, the cruel hobble one was given, one relaxes. Not into mediocrity but into a kind of hurricane's eye. One forgets the present age and the abstractions that make it up and turns to the work at hand, out of which some honest (even lasting) good may come.

*Mary Kinzie*
*Evanston, Illinois*
*1 February 1993*

## NOTES

1. F. T. Prince to John Ashbery, 1 June 1958. Among the Schuyler/Ashbery papers at the Mandeville Department of Special Collections, University of California at San Diego. MSS 78, box 1, folder 13.

2. Iris Murdoch, "Against Dryness: A Polemical Sketch," *Encounter* 16 (1961): 16–20.

3. J. V. Cunningham, "The Judge Is Fury" (1947), in *The Exclusions of a Rhyme: Poems and Epigrams* (Chicago: Swallow Press, 1960), p. 43.

# Contents

# From "'How Could Fools Get Tired!'"

Poets, even good ones, are not writing good poetry all the time. Sometimes they are warming up or cooling down or just maintaining muscle tone. One somewhat daffy habit among poets who are not writing poetry is the kind of posturing that might be described as acting lovable. This might lead to whimsy or nonsense literature were it not for the evident strain with which some poets have to labor to be light-hearted. Further, there is often an existential chic, a flavoring of Kafka, which these poets of the offhanded and the fanciful try to imitate—as if runes and paradox were so regular a feature of their thought that they could rise, in any slack moment, from the casually available, heterogeneous dreck.

Michael Brownstein in *Strange Days Ahead* gives an apt description of the dreck from which his emblems are mined: "a state / of strange mess bordering on ecstasy / and, to the south, lunacy. / To the north snores calm maturity. . . . In the east rumbles power. / The sweet machine. Amphetamine." A rather nice interior rhyme, that—surely better than some of his others: *water/otter, Bucket/fuck it, Kyoto/sofa*. But the "state of mind / bordering on infancy" in his poem "Geography" sug-

Review of Michael Brownstein, *Strange Days Ahead* (Calais, VT: Z Press, 1975); Albert Goldbarth, *Comings Back* (Garden City, NY: Doubleday, 1976); Ted Hughes, *Moon-Whales* (New York: Viking, 1976); *The New Naked Poetry: Recent American Poetry in Open Forms*, ed. Stephen Berg and Robert Mezey (New York: Macmillan/Bobbs-Merrill, 1976); John Balaban, *After Our War* (Pittsburgh: University of Pittsburgh Press, 1974); Lucien Stryk, *Selected Poems* (Chicago: Swallow Press, 1976).

gests a poetic persona that will manage to take *itself* seriously while everything else it touches is taken as casually as possible. In some loose sense it is a Song of My American Self: Cadillacs, ice packs, stockbrokers with cigars and—a rendition of the purer of its products gone transparent if not mad—"The corkscrew comes alive under the dining room rug / The Bronx creamery reflected in old Shoshone eyes." "The bank," Brownstein asserts, "is made astounding, ineffable, inexorable / By the people who fill it . . . a squad of olive-drab sideburn otherness / And plumbers."

Sometimes Brownstein's non sequiturs are framed by standard discourse, as in the conditional: "And if, as Goethe said, architecture is frozen music / Then it sounds today as if a pack of rats / Is slowly being tortured to death." Sometimes in broken syntax without particularly having proven that in poetry he has found it, he writes about losing it:

> Why is it sometimes
> I feel good
> Sometimes I feel bad
> And the times I don't feel at all
> Times I don't feel at all drift—
> I can't even say this—
> Drift past my window
> Because the window in this poem
> Is in this poem
> But hold it, a second
> Hold it
> Just hold it

And sometimes, as in the title poem, Brownstein races toward surrealism, leaving assertion to the gaps between such lines as "Oceanic push-ups" and "Flavored green thumbprints," or between "Rollo mine flavored sweep-o-mints" and "The chicken gun." Presumably all of these things exist, chicken guns, sweep-o-mints, and "target flippers"—not as real things (few poets demand of us such naïveté), but as verbal toys interesting for the writer. Whatever associations join them are buried so that, prevented from taking pleasure in the structure of the thought, we are left only with the possibility of pleasure in the pieces. Few of the pieces, however, have the grace, inventiveness, or seductive sense of lost clue one might expect from a dismantled mosaic. Although there are some gradations—"the dental tartar of respect" being far sillier than the "alien / Corn of congratulation."

Whether he is parodying a well-worn moment in a Keats ode or Blake's four-square city, Brownstein is intent on putting the tradition down. In its place he gives us, at worst, a mad ephemera ("the succulent baby checkerboard we pour milk on") and, at best, phrases that would, if mastered in Russian or Czech, be of some use when traveling: "I am angry. / You are here. / She is gone." His book is evidence of the serious or professional flakiness that in various homely chunks now seems to constitute the American avant-garde.

Albert Goldbarth's much longer, more garrulous and ambitious book, *Comings Back*, is also wearisomely avant-garde and just as determinedly whimsical or off-guarded. Although the range of poems is broader, both backward in history and laterally in the exploration of voices, Goldbarth's assumption is little different from Brownstein's: namely, that our dislocated musings are the repositories of significant inner logic, that the gaps between our thoughts are where true sense is to be found, and that our jumbled nightmares, faithfully presented in all their jumble, embody ultimate meaning. From the kindliest perspective, one might say the ultimate meaning was simply that we *are* jumbled and dream-driven creatures. From a perspective less kind, which the unabashed smugness of Goldbarth's coterie attitude may invite, ultimate meaning may be a much more limited matter of the poet's indulgence toward the sensitive, disaffected cronies to whom he addresses his verse epistles.

In a poem that begins "Dear Liz: A dream. For which I offer / No exegesis," an old Scot appears, "his arms, / from the wheeling, were terraced; his tongue / revolved in his brogue like a gerbil." "And in that moment," writes Goldbarth (whatever it was), "I knew, Liz, how / it would turn out okay for people / like us." In the long "Letter to Tony: Suitable for Presentation as a Gift," Goldbarth writes to console his friend for the break with Sharon and throws around a great deal of

Egyptian lore because together he, Sharon, and Tony had seen the scarab at an Egyptian exhibit. Leaping briskly "Over the winking penis of Thoth," Goldbarth lands on the emblem for this looping, tasteless coprolith—the dung beetle. To cheer Tony up, he elaborates the various ways in which the sun rises like "A ball of shit," and jubilantly calls what results "This art: these smear gifts renewed at every birth." He is rather like the high school cutup, barking out juvenile obscenities, then aestheticizing them.

No patently sexual or scatological motifs are present in Ted Hughes's book, *Moon-Whales*, but the poems here suffer just as Goldbarth's do from trying to be cutely hard-headed. Unlike Brownstein and Goldbarth, however, the saccharin quality is alien to Hughes, who never entirely masks a savage grimace. Hughes is often trying to write metrical, rhymed verse. The eeriness of the poems is that they are not even serviceable doggerel. In "Moon-Marriage," various animals appear in dreams and announce that they are married to you,

> Or maybe deep in your sleep a mountain looms
> With rumbling and lightning and misty glooms,
> Whispering, "Do you love me
> As much as I love you?" And you wake
> With your nose bleeding, and all one terrible ache
> Like a worn-out mountaineer,
> And still feeling the precipices near.

The anguish of the patched-out rhymes and stumbling rhythms is evenly reflected by the embarrassment of the images: "Now harmonicas on the moon are humorous, / The tunes produce German Measles, but the speckles are more numerous." The dracula vine is a moon-pet that transforms trash into fruit: "So this is a useful pet / And loyal if well-treat. / But if you treat it badly / It will wander off sadly // Till somebody with more garbage than you / gives its flowers something to do." One would prefer the more innocent, mild, and accomplished poetry of Milne, the marvelous ghostliness of Lear, and certainly the ballad wit of a Plomer or a Betjeman to the messy versification and sluggish monsters here. Even the Leonard Baskin drawings that decorate the Hughes book are a bit thin. Perhaps Hughes should try someplace more down to earth—say the licorice fields at Pontefract.

*The New Naked Poetry: Recent American Poetry in Open Forms* suggests that poetry can be equally dreary when it tries to be oracular. Dedicated "to the memory of the great American poet, Pablo Neruda" (Neruda was Chilean), the volume is printed in a sans serif type that blinds one after a time, and the format is the framing of a batch of poems with the poet's picture at the beginning and a prose statement from most at the end. None of these facts is very reassuring; but the structure or rationale for the anthology is harder to divine. How do Rexroth's translations from the *Greek Anthology* make common cause with Ginsberg's endless syndetic chants? The title's stipulation that the poetry be "recent" is followed, with some obvious exceptions, and becomes a laming principle where writers like Bly, Simpson, and Rich are concerned, since their earlier work was a great deal more substantial than their later. From the vague requirement that these be poems in "open forms" comes, I would guess, the prevalence of the long, prophetic, unreadable poem, the letter poem (that is, barely cadenced prose), the ragtag poem (lines dispersed all over the page), the minimal poem of very short lines (preferably irregular), and finally, the poem that just maunders on. The editors recoil from explaining the "naked" as well: "[W]e are not theoreticians. We write the stuff, and here, in order to make a little money, to enlarge the audience for poets we love," and to produce yet another college textbook, they have published a successor to the *Naked Poetry* of eight years ago. "It is," they say, "for the reader, the listener, and not machines and paradigms to decide if the poem rings true."

Fair enough. Although the following lines are out of context, they register some of the false knells I hear: "The interior of the room was as clear / As a glimpse of brain surgery"; "Introspective as a leper"; "riding anguish as Tartars ride mares"; "Kitchen-windows like heads / Bandaged for toothache"; "mothers' vulvas made baseballs to their lust"; "It is because we have new packaging for smoked oysters that bomb holes appear in the paddies"; "fuck fanon nixon / and malcolm fuck the revolution fuck freedom fuck / the whole mothafuckin thing"; "I smile again, just because I can"; "The anguish of a naked body is more terrible / To bear than God"; a baby at birth is "clotted with celestial cheesiness, flowing / with the astral violet / of the underlife"; "damerging a nuv. A nerb. / the present dented of the U / nighted stayd. States"; "Star-striped scoundrelesque flag-dopers"; "CRYING / all these passt, / losst / years"; "Love-apples cramp you sideways / with sudden emptiness"; "the oak-borers of Ivy League schools' mistletoe masters." As Frank O'Hara writes in an included poem, "this may sound tendentious, but it's lyrical."

It is a relief to surface from these mixed metaphors and self-important harangues and come upon the good-tempered funniness of O'Hara and Kenneth Koch; the sometimes mannered but ingenious later Merwin and the quiet, steady William Stafford are equally easy. But the general confusion of mind and shapelessness of the "art" here are so depressing that not even some of the more riotous prose apologias can cheer one up. Whether they're throwing around science (the three-brain theory of human melioration), Freudian analysis, or other people's poetry, it seems very few of these poets think carefully even when off-duty. Most of them honor Williams and Whitman as their models. There is, accordingly, much talk of the variable foot and the valvèd voice, breath, inner rhythms, incantations—and much more talk of inspiration, being misunderstood, saying it straight, getting it down, and getting it right. Along with "rightness" comes the question of topic, what one ought to write about, and my favorite essay explaining what poets ought to write about is the following:

> the male lyric poet ... builds in his work the body of his mother.... [In so doing] the poet establishes a sexual relationship with his own work.... The fact that so many lyric poets die young ... suggests that they cannot duplicate in their work the lower half of the mother's body.... [B]reaking into syntax, an advance that makes poetry possible, comes about ... in con-

nection with attempts to deal with the separation from the mother at about the age of 1½.

There is a land, Kafka reminds us, where no one sleeps because no one ever gets tired, and the reason they don't is because they're fools: "'Don't fools get tired?' 'How could fools get tired!'" The sacrament of comedy, now, is supposedly celebrated if you can (a) live long enough, (b) break into syntax and stay there a while (c) like Magritte, putting the fish part of the mermaid on top. And no snickering—that is what we do at "bastard comedy which has somehow short-circuited the moment of the truly comic." We laugh at Kenneth Koch's poetry "for the same reason we laugh at jokes [!], because we are spared the expenditure of energy necessary to deal with anxieties aroused by feelings, and this excess of energy can emerge in the smile." We are therefore referred by the writer to a poem in this volume called "The Teeth Mother Naked at Last," a war poem that, for all its other flaws (those smoked oysters), has to its credit that it has nothing to do with the lower half of the mother's body. A sample:

> I know that books are tired of us.
> I *know* they are chaining the Bible to chairs.
> Books don't want to remain in the same room with us anymore.
>
> New Testaments are escaping . . . dressed as women . . . they go off after dark.
> And Plato! Plato . . . Plato wants to go backwards. . . .
> He wants to hurry back up the river of time, so he can end as some blob of flesh rotting on an Australian beach.
>
> Why are they dying? I have written this so many times.
> They are dying because the President has opened a Bible again.

John Balaban's *After Our War* is more circumspect than most of the naked poetry in its social criticisms as well as in its forms, and because written by a firsthand observer, what he has to say about the war in Vietnam makes the President opening his Bible look more and more flimsy. Balaban uses catalogues precise in visual as well as emotional effects. In "Midnight at Phoenix Island in the Mekong," for example, the sewage-filled water turns into

> moonshoals swallowing every human token:
> Roman coin, Thai celadon, sundered Cham navies,
> black opium bricks, tribute girls chokered in gold,
> French bibles and cannon, spittle and shit.
> A nighthawk bleats and skims the inky trees.

Southeast Asia's whole muddy, glinting history is told in those lines.

If at times the Hemingway-interlude-in-war poem can be suspiciously flat, Balaban is also able to turn the flat observation of "Polluted Place" into these deft and sinister lines: "A heron swooped over it / low and darkly / like a scowl, but would not land. / Oil slicked the surface of the ooze. // The trees crept away from its banks." Even if the poem of large statement is sometimes not as strong as that of the small, not all of Balaban's ambitious works are improperly elevated. In the strange mixture of virtue and vice, "Pentangle," an image to which Leavis might object as strenuously as he did to Shelley's clouds like leaves shook from the tangled boughs of Heaven and Ocean—namely, one that creates several pictures impossible to imagine all at the same time—will place ancient warships beside autumnal decay in arresting lines: "In October, triremes of leaves / choke the harbored heavens / and suffocate the foam strokes." Although leaves falling through air, while not regularly arranged in three tiers, could remind us of the lines of oars working from a trireme, the leaves as oars would not suffocate the strokes they made. The image indicates, however, the writer's ability to think simultaneously visually, analogically, and emotionally while at the same time keeping an ear out for the smooth and almost impersonal voice of verbal rightness. Even on the basis of the October triremes I would claim for this poet intelligence and a natural visual discipline, the rare potential for retreat behind achieved work.

Even when Balaban is patently drawing upon his experience

in the late sixties as a young man fit to fight in Vietnam, he is able to extrapolate his own situation — for example, waiting to be shipped over—into lines whose universal poignancy naturally flows into a quotation from a classical lament:

> Time once. But our time will not
> circle back with the river valley seasons
> where the Shenandoah licks the face
> of the Potomac. In the morning
> there will be no waking at your side.
> Alone but for three sullen, dry-faced
> .sisters, I rock and creak my chair
> on the peeling stoop. I wait to go.
> *"Rura valete iterum tuque optima Lydia salve."*

The kind of analogical thought manifest in "Pentangle," moving back and forth between the poet's time and Vergil's, between America and Vietnam, comparing science to murder or vision to guilt, is a basic structure in *After Our War*. As Balaban suggests in the title of a poem comparing Saigon and Pittsburgh, many of his poems adapt the purely verbal concept of the palindrome (something that reads the same backwards as forwards) to a metaphoric posture of some interpretive power that will conclude in the elegies. "Along the Mekong," section 1, also suggests reversible connections between the chemical maiming of laboratory animals and of the "hare-lipped, tusk-toothed" Vietnamese children, and in the poem's second section, in language too wounded to be humble, a more elaborate cultural palindrome appears. The rubble of war in this jungle country could *not* be conveyed by any reporter or cook because the listing of casualties in nature must reflect the attachment of the spectator. By this revision of the trope of art as mirror to the world (less Shakespeare perhaps than Stendhal), Balaban makes a strong political statement about his representative guilt that, sagely and quietly, counters the overwriting that precedes:

> Catfish flip for air.
> Sunfish, gutted and gilled, cheek plates snipped.
> . . . . . . . . . . . . . . . . . . . . . . . . . . . . . . . . . . . . . .

Pig halves knotted from fist-size hooks. Sorcerers,
palmists, and, under a tarp: thick incense, candles.
Why, a reporter, or a cook, could write this poem
if he had learned dictation. But what if I said,
simply suggested, that all this blood fleck,
muscle rot, earth root and earth leaf, scraps
of glittery scales, fine white grains, fast talk,
gut grime, crab claws, bright light, sweetest smells
—Said: a human self; a mirror held up before.

The twelve-page elegy for David Gitelson, a civilian agricul-
tural advisor shot by the Vietcong, is such a mirror, held up
before. "The Gardenia in the Moon" juxtaposes Gitelson's offi-
cial reports that begin with infected apple trees and end with
pleas against the senseless and officially disavowed bombing of
civilians, with city views of beggars, flower-choked French gov-
ernment palaces now used by Americans, and young mothers
abandoning their children to solicit their protectors. The poem
begins in that state of double reference we have seen in
"Pentangle," but it nevertheless preserves the structure of el-
egy: detailing the confusion in one's own life, and specifically in
the disconnected state of bereavement, in order to yield these
up to the invocation of the lost being who joins the divided
doubles and condemnatory palimpsests back together.

Lucien Stryk's substantial and various work both in original
poetry and in Zen translation will remind us of another kind
of *via negativa* illustrated by the Hasidic parable about the
pupil who was supposed to fast and became thirsty. He was
about to drink from a pool when he considered that he had
come this far, he could hold out a bit longer. Then he thought
he was becoming full of pride about his refusal, decided again
to drink, and suddenly realized that he was no longer thirsty.
When he crossed his teacher's door, all the rabbi said to him
was "Patchwork." He had, in other words, tried to earn a
claim to virtue where appetite in fact was in control, even by
its temporary lapse. "My failing in poetry," wrote Stryk about
his first three volumes, "was the result ... of a grave misun-
derstanding concerning the very purpose of art." The Zen
masters he was translating at the time "did not think of them-

selves as 'poets' at all; rather they were attempting to express in verse nothing less than the Zen spirit," writing "poems without any pretension to 'art.' "

As there are many splendid poems in Stryk's first three books, and many slack ones after, let us assume this realization about the artlessness of art that seeks to divest itself of banality to be a statement about the entirety of his endeavor. And let's assume that artless mediation between world and eye is the virtue sought in many poems, while the thirst for links to the self and for the comforts of poetic role and poetic sound is the appetite that, even when dormant, sometimes undermines the enterprise. The argument between these two, virtue and appetite, seems to me fairly constant throughout Stryk's *Selected Poems*. Its resolutions are as tentative and breathtaking as are his fragile syllabic structures as stays against the throng of cadences:

> There are
> Days when I
> Am troubled by an image of the house,
>
> Laden, rootless, like a tinseled tree,
> Suddenly
> Torn to a thousand scribbled leaves and borne off
>
> By the wind, then to be gathered and patched
> Whole again,
> Or of the thing going up in smoke
>
> And I, the paper dreamer, wide awake.
>
> ("Oeuvre")

Certainly, he resists. For what a simple thing it would have been, and how obvious, to remove the "and" between "leaves" and "borne," to remove "the" before "wind," to substitute a two-syllable iambic past participle for "patched," to insert "whole" before "thing," and in doing so to strike the gong a great deal harder. By making the choices we see him having made in "Oeuvre," Stryk not only takes our attention away from the line as unit, but reveals as well a longer rhythmic unit that takes here about seven lines to express itself. The long lines waver between iambic and trochaic pentameters on the one hand, and a nine- and eleven-syllable count on the other; and the refusal to determine between these schemata while holding himself clearly poised between the rhythm and the count is Stryk's precarious metric discipline, one amounting to self-effacement.

When the effacement is carried to a further extreme, that is, when coupled with an uncanny ability to look while he is writing, Stryk can scan that small space beyond himself where being-in-the-world occurs. He is speaking about the fifteenth-century painter Sesshu's rock garden in the temple of Joeiji:

> Distance between the rocks,
>     Half the day
> In shadow, is the distance
>
> Between the man who thinks
>     And the man
> Who thinks he thinks: wait,
>
> Like a brain, the garden,
>     Thinking when
> It is thought. Otherwise
>
> A stony jumble, merely that,
>     Laid down there
> To stud our emptiness.
>
> ("Zen: The Rocks of Sesshu, III")

There is nothing sure here. The threat of a mere studding of pieces looms behind the arduous circularities in which the insight is framed, and yet the entire eight sections of the poem record one of life's great experiences: an order earned by meditation.

The influence of Zen may stand as token for the paring and reduction that Stryk has taken to heart. It removes him into a realm of satisfying deprivation—the visual item in solitude, the transcendent, bare particular. In some poems, the pruning is so severe that, while syntax is preserved, it seems skeletal. The emphasis shifts away from predication. Only a few bare branches, haggard nouns, icy verbs, fraying adjectives, mark the place where filler might have been:

> Afternoons, they
> Lean across the tables, burning,
>
> To watch the years slip away like freighters
> > Down the seaways.
> And there remain, knowing the worst
>
> Of inland days, the rot, the sloth,
> > The ennui, to
> Tramp in dream the unmarked shore.
>
> ("Escale")

If the focus here is too general and the distance from eye to world too great, so that the passage seems adjectival and random, still the diction is peculiarly pure. But these are initiating lines for Stryk, not what he's capable of at best, but ones that reveal his methods. In more achieved poems like "Awakening: Homage to Hakuin, Zen Master, 1685–1768," the stark residuum of thought when all opportunity for digression has been pared away reveals a form more intact: "I balance the round stone / in my palm, / turn it full circle, / slowly, in the late sun, / spring to now. / Severe compression, // like a troubled head, / stings my hand. / It falls. A small dust rises." "Spring to now"—that brief torque of monosyllables—makes the stone into a cosmos turning on its axis, and in that metaphor troubling his head, the round stone turns again, into an emblem of the mind that cannot be pressed further or held longer.

I take it that in *Selected Poems* Stryk desires to be permitted to say a few things about how poetry is made. Not all of these self-referential statements interest us. Those that do, "Zen: The Rocks of Sesshu," "The Duckpond," "Awakening," and "Morning," are those in which the syllabic strength is greatest and in which, perhaps paradoxically, the descriptive appetite has been most sharply curbed: "[E]verything waits / to happen. The paper on the desk / is like a distant / sunlit pool, my pen / an indolent bather, weary of all."

# The Music of Overemphasis

Frank Bidart in both *Golden State* (1973) and *The Book of the Body* (1977) is bent on reaching the resonating center of experience, whether the language appropriate to it is witty, simple, or abstract. He has assembled collections of poems that fit together in thematic patterns that support the primary trait of the poems—urgency. The poems' form belies their necessity, however, because they look so random or approximate on the page. Compared with many a writer's minimal lines or some others' long Pindaric alternations, Bidart's work is somewhat unattractive to the eye. Farrar, Straus has provided him with a wider page, making every effort to compensate for his irregularities. But the effect of the dropped lines and indentations, of the capitals and italics, and of the semicolons and commas directly preceding dashes,—or succeeding them—, all make me wonder what inner rhythms he is trying to catch, and why he resorts to typographic oddities.

Bidart's form is based on double voices; the voices of the sufferers are counterpointed by the dry, magisterial tones of the clinicians and wardens. In "The Arc," a dramatic monologue spoken by a man who has lost an arm, we come upon these instructions:

> 1. Always bandage *firmly*. The pressure should be constant over the entire stump with greatest pressure near the tip to attempt to make the stump cone-shaped.
> . . . . . . . . . . . .

---

First published in different form in 1979.

3. Wash bandage with mild soap. . . . DO NOT WRING! . . .
   DO NOT STRETCH OR IRON!
4. Change the stump sock daily. Wash . . . DO NOT
   WRING!

These instructions (like all official pronouncements that stan-
dardize the grotesque) are parodic, overemphatic in the
wrong places ("DO NOT WRING!"), and hopelessly tactless
when the injury itself is referred to: "2. If stump starts to
*throb*, remove bandage at once. . . . Inspect the skin of your
stump daily for any blisters, spots or sores and report them."
Thus the bureaucratic mind condescends to pain and loss:
Clearly it won't do any good to report them. The Bidart
speaker is less interested in the care of his stump, in making
it properly cone-shaped, than he is in eradicating in himself
the memory of his arm and of all the things he saw in the
world from the vantage of a whole, two-armed being. He
dreams of his stump as a tombstone on which his own birth
date and the date of the car crash form an "arc" of accident
within design.

   In the mid-sixties, taking an even more aggressive attitude
toward the macabre instruction manual, W. D. Snodgrass had
written:

> Take the first two fingers of this hand:
> Fork them out—kind of a "V for Victory"—
> . . . . . . . . . . . . . . . . . . . . . . . . . . . . . . . . . . .
> And jam them into the eyes of your enemy.
> You have to do this hard. Very hard. Then press
> . . . . . . . . . . . . . . . . . . . . . . . . . . . . . . . . . . .
> Both fingers down around the cheekbone
> And setting your foot high into the chest
> . . . . . . . . . . . . . . . . . . . . . . . . . . . . . . . . . . .
> You must call up every strength you own
> And you can rip off the whole facial mask.

Snodgrass weaves into the career sergeant's lecture (in those
ellipses) slightly revised passages from an essay by the soli-
tary philosopher who wrote, "We must in no way despise

technology"—Baruch Spinoza. In Snodgrass's slightly adapted pentameter, the Spinoza essay begins, "After experience had taught me that all the ordinary / Surroundings of social life are futile and vain. . . ." The philosophical voice coincides with the bland yet horrifying combat voice at the point where the phrase *to preserve one's being* in the Spinoza lines agrees psychologically with the more immediate cruelty in the sergeant's:

> . . . I resolved to inquire
> *Take the first two fingers, etc.*
> Whether there might be something whose discovery
> Would grant me supreme, unending happiness.
> *And jam them, etc.*
> No virtue can be thought to have priority
> Over this endeavor to preserve one's being.
> *Both fingers around the cheekbone, etc.*

Spinoza is used to devastating purpose, supporting from an Olympian vantage the small grisly deaths closer in. The two parts of the Snodgrass poem nod to each other in partial complicity and partial ignorance across the poet's rage. It is Frost's lesson about the changing valence of experience brought to the pitch of the battlefield, prison camp, and asylum: One can preserve one's own meaning only by rejecting the world's meaning—and vice versa. For Bidart's speaker in "The Arc," as for Snodgrass in "After Experience," the task is to keep oblivion at hand as a medicine for the shudder of thought.

Bidart's one-armed man stays sane by forgetting—by recoiling from interpretation. The narrator says that every morning when he wakes he tries to convince himself that his arm isn't there: "Then I try to convince myself it is." His mother's delusion at McLean's Hospital near Boston (she "believed the painting of a snow-scene above her bed / had been placed there by the doctor to make her feel cold") is wistfully compared with his own trouble: "I tell myself / 'Insanity is the insistence on meaning.' " But refusing to overinterpret as his mother had done, body takes over from mind. He tries to have sex with a Vietnam vet but, when the time comes, he "forgot why / a body can make me feel horny." He remembers a patient on his mother's ward who was determined, by refusing to wear clothes, to evade identity: "I only saw her once," the speaker says, but "even in my mind, / sweating / she wears a body." The world seems populated by paradoxes.

The main dilemma in "The Arc" inheres in the attempt to erase the paralyzing awareness of having a body that is wrong, partly amputated, ungovernable by mind; but when the speaker escapes to Europe or, in the following passage, to art, he inevitably faces not only unwilled travesties of his problem ("his *arms* lightly touching," "directed by the angel's *arms*," "his *arms* lightly touching the globe"), but the sterner emblems of what will not work even in art and dream. Michelangelo's book of the body had the painter-sculptor's beaten face for colophon, just as the Bidart speaker has his stump. In his marvelous, idiosyncratic homage to Michelangelo's drawing *The Dream*, Bidart sees masks as discarded selves that cannot be discarded: They return as the Deadly Sins of identity, and recall the painter's self-signature in the mural of the *Last Judgment*, the torso of the aging but muscular Hephaistos beneath the face of a goblin; this figure,

his arms lightly touching the globe,
all the masks at last lying dead beneath him,

is wakened by an angel
                    hovering above him
. . . . . . . . . . . . . . . . . . . . . . . . . . . . . . . . . . . .
the angel's trumpet directed by the angel's arms,
the two figures connected by a trumpet,
wakened to the World ranged round him,
which is his dream, as well as Sin:

*Sex. Identity. History. Family.*
*Affection. Obsession. Chance.*
                                        —the seven

Deadly Sins, spirit
implicating itself in matter, only able to know itself
by what it has done in Time,—

are all ranged round him, the angel
waking him to himself . . . his arms lightly touching the globe.

Perhaps it is merely the verbal echo ("masks at last lying
dead") that, in the context of the doubling of voice—the
instruction manual and the spirit's answer—reminds me of
Snodgrass ("you can rip off the whole facial mask"). But
there is a deeper issue in the Bidart poem that strengthens
the similarity to Snodgrass—the idea, as Bidart phrases it, of
"spirit / implicating itself in matter, only able to know itself /
by what it has done in Time." The Spinoza voice of retire-
ment, of self-containment, comes back to the bedrock of be-
ing; the dream comes back to the Deadly Sins of accident
and opportunity—what the soul commits in Time by merely
existing.

When Bidart's increasingly mythical one-armed figure re-
turns to Europe, the stage of exile and self-confrontation, he
encounters a number of tests. He sees a boy running with his
dog; the dog is missing one foreleg: "I felt that I too must
erase my past, / that I could, *must* pretend (almost / as an
experiment) I had never had more / than one arm." Then he
realizes that, despite being happy for a few weeks after that,
all the associations called vividly forth by Paris are wrong:
They are associations made by a man who forgot he wasn't
whole. "I had to try to cut from my brain / my phantom hand /
which still gets cramps," and in order to do so the man thinks
of Paris: "still the city of Louis XVI and / Robespierre, how
blood, amputation, and rubble // give her dimension, reso-
nancy, and grace." "The Arc" abruptly and a bit sloppily closes
on this "comfort" derived from a blatant historical fatalism
nobody will believe could help the amputee for long. In other
words, the finale of the poem solves nothing—a fact I pre-
sume the poet knows, although the sheer conclusiveness of
the lines makes me wary.

The close of the poem "Ellen West" poses a different sort of
problem for the reader, inasmuch as the woman the analyst
Ludwig Binswanger referred to under this fictitious name did
in fact kill herself after being released from the last mental

institution she visited. She had a metabolic tendency to gain weight and had for ten years been terrified of becoming fat. Bidart correctly notes her "childish / dread of eating," her daydreams of enormous quantities of sweets, her obsession with bread. But it is also important to realize, as Bidart does, that what terrified Ellen West in the last three years of her life was neither eating nor food, since those fears had already been transformed into a pattern of extreme self-denial; what she came to fear was hunger, and the syndrome of its reappearance even after stuffing herself. Her dread of eating was eventually not fear of increase but fear of ensuing hunger, and the gap or abyss in the self this hunger directly denoted and aggravated.

Like the man in "The Arc," Ellen West is struggling to overcome a lack in the body, a psychic version of a gap below the elbow. In her case, the gap is represented by her hunger— her dread of it and her simultaneous failure to realize in fasting and emetics the etheriality of pure spirit. Rather than becoming more free of her body, she is chained to its necessities. One of the most remarkable additions Bidart makes to the Binswanger case study is a brilliant three-and-a-half page memorial to the opera singer Maria Callas, whose voice gave out when she lost weight. "The *tapeworm*," says Ellen West in Bidart's increasingly emphatic typography, "was her *soul*."

> Perhaps her mind,
> ravenous, still insatiable, sensed
> that to struggle with the *shreds* of a voice
>
> must make her artistry subtler, more refined,
> more capable of expressing humiliation,
> rage, betrayal . . .

Listening to Callas sing *Tosca*, Ellen thinks she is watching the singer's own autobiography: "'Art has *repaid* me LIKE THIS?' " Callas's was

> an art; skill;
> virtuosity

miles distant from the usual soprano's
athleticism,—
                    the usual musician's dream
of virtuosity *without* content . . .

But at last Callas is caught within the parentheses of her re-
corded career; hearing her now, says Ellen, even Callas her-
self would know that her style had begun to date a little, and
would feel that

she probably would *not* do a trill in
*exactly* that way,—
                    that the whole sound, atmosphere,
*dramaturgy* of her recordings
have just slightly become those of the past . . .

Ellen believes that at last her soul must have whispered to
Callas, "*The only way / to escape / the History of Styles / is not to have
a body.*"
    When I first read Frank Bidart's poems of the body, espe-
cially the frankly autobiographical sequences ("Golden State"
in the earlier volume, "Elegy" and "The Book of the Body" in
the present one), I thought that his habit of *landing* on words
("This *I* is anterior / to name; gender; action; / fashion; /
MATTER ITSELF,—") was his way of rendering that speech-
rhythm in several senses gay: eager, wry, exuberant, faintly
British and tart, sometimes tortuously, sometimes subtly off-
key or counterpointed to expected emphasis. I thought I had
remembered Richard Howard, especially in *Untitled Subjects*,
doing something very similar. But Howard doesn't play the
emphasis quite so hard, and furthermore, his Victorian mono-
logists seem to come by their pacing and their pedantry as
part of the common inheritance of the age; Henry James
would be a good example of a Victorian writer who allots
strong, portentous beats to plain words.
    Then I thought: *No*, being gay (as the truer model for this
oddly paced, oddly emphatic voice would say) was not *just* it.
I'm thinking, of course, of Randall Jarrell, that repeater of
abstractions that have a certain familiar warmth in his verse
(pain, darkness, wisdom, knowledge—see Bidart's "spirit / im-

plicating itself in matter"), of Jarrell, who made overemphasis
a touchstone of emotion:

> "But I'm a *good* girl."
>
> "Oh, it's not *right!*"
>
> "No, that is not *just* it."
>
> What do I *really* look like?
> I don't know.
> Not really.
> > *Really.*
>
> They *said* he went to Scotland.
>
> I got *everything* wrong.
>
> And yet it wasn't *interesting* . . .
> —It was worse than impossible, it was a joke.
>
> How young I seem; I *am* exceptional.
>
> "I don't *know!* I don't *know!*"

Although it seems to me that Bidart handles the emphasis less
dramatically than Jarrell, there is a tendency for his style to
become sentimental too:

> How can I say this?
> > I think my psychiatrist
>
> *likes* me.
> . . . . . . . .
> the *bewilderment*, unease;
> the somehow always
> tentative, suspended judgment . . .
>
> —however *much* you tried (and, clearly,
> you *did* try)
> > ("Golden State")

> the *solution* was to forget
> that I had ever had an arm.
> > *The lost arm had never existed.*
> . . . . . . . . . . . . . . . . . . . . . . . . . . . . . . . . . . . . . . . . . . . .
> —Blindness. Blankness.
> A friend said, "I've hurt so many . . ." And

*for* what?

        to what *end?*—

. . . . . . . . . . . . . . . . . . . . . . .

  the un-mappable mountain
of FEELING

                          ("The Book of the Body")

Perhaps the test of any manner is in knowing when not to use it; thus the sudden nightmare effect of a Bidart poem entirely free of his customary exclamations and syncopated beats. The effect is similar to the doubling of voice mentioned earlier. Just as the instructions for the care of the stump and the case-study inserts of Ellen West's doctors baffle and intensify the overwrought monologues by repeating the speaker's obsessions in a more acceptable "realistic" voice, so the *loud* words made vivid by italics are in turn baffled by the *un*emphatic voice:

> I am asleep, dreaming a terrible dream, so I awake,
> and want to call my father to ask if, just
> for a short time, the dog can come to stay with me.
>
> But the light next to my bed won't light:
> I press and press the switch. Touching the phone,
> I can't see to dial the numbers. Can I learn how to keep
> the dog in my apartment? In the dark, trying
> a second light, I remember
> I always knew these machines would fail me.
>                                Then I awake,
> remember my father and the dog are dead,
> the lights in that room do not go on.

                          ("Elegy," IV, "Light")

When I read about the lights that do not go on, I see the afterimage of strong statement hovering over the words: do *not* go on, do not go *on*, do not *go on*. In the same way (if this can still be called an afterimage), the mildness of voice to which Bidart occasionally resorts hovers over the most emphatic passages, erasing the italics in

        the way each *gladly*
        put the *food* the other had offered *into his mouth*—;

so that we see and read without surprised punctuation, odd typography, perhaps even without line breaks: "[T]he way each gladly put the food the other had offered into his mouth, I knew they slept together."

    In his eccentric way, Bidart comes close to Frost's use of the Romantic moment, the one out of which larger meanings flow. One of Bidart's ways of achieving this synthesis of the temporal with the timeless is to make us read the emphatic words with a pure and requisite disinterest, in order, eventually, that we read the colorless statement with a peculiar emphasis. I think he teaches us something about the way we sound. He has in a sense parodied his personal intonations so that his poems become large, impersonal, and endlessly resonant. Being caught up in the middle of things means something different for Robert Frost than for Frank Bidart, since for Bidart it means being caught up in the middle of *things*, Sex, Identity, Affection, Chance, unable to **LET GO**.

# From "A Generation of Silver"

Although art must address the emotions, it should also burn with the impersonal fire of a possession that has many names—language, imagination, anamnesis, inspiration, form. This is the part of a literary work in which style and truth have been wrested out of a living tradition.

A literary tradition is alive insofar as it promotes, in a body of poetry, the engagement of the writer with the greatest breadth of human endeavor and the greatest particularity of individual vision. Above all, good poetry is written consciously, even if it also desires contact with realms believed unconscious: Poetry requires that the writer serve an apprenticeship to technique. All three metrical prosodies in postclassical European poetry (accentual, syllabic, and accentual-syllabic), as well as the nonmetrical prosody of free verse, ask the writer to juggle two unequal "measures": syntax and line. When syntax and line habitually coincide, yet another measuring device will be needed for inequality—in accentual-syllabic verse, this third device may be the implicit punning of rhymes or greater syntactic condensation, and in free verse it might be some disequilibrium in mood or narration between lines assumed (in this case) to be formed of syntactically whole

---

Review of Marilyn Hacker, *Taking Notice* (New York: Knopf, 1980); William Virgil Davis, *One Way to Reconstruct the Scene* (New Haven: Yale University Press, 1980); Heather McHugh, *A World of Difference* (Boston: Houghton Mifflin, 1981); Gregory Orr, *The Red House* (New York: Harper & Row, 1980); James McMichael, *Four Good Things* (Boston: Houghton Mifflin, 1980); Alicia Ostriker, *The Mother/Child Papers* (Santa Monica: Momentum Press, 1980).

phrases. (Many writers of free verse lineate by phrase alone, so that the free-verse line does nothing the syntax of English does not already do.)

Coincidence and discontinuity are the twinned resources of technical mastery in poetry, and of imaginative mastery, or wit. Without coincidence (based on sound or syntax), no discontinuity is possible, whether rhetorical (like zeugma) or prosodic (like enjambment). And, most important, without discontinuity in some form, coincidence can have no force.

More embattled than the question of form is the question of feeling. Given the variability of poetic subject over time, and the cultural shifts that erode some standards (like the "poetic kinds") and substitute new and sometimes more *ad hoc* ones, it is absurd to claim that all poetry has one enduring theme. Any definition of poetry that would try to account for both Frank O'Hara and Homer would perforce become so general as to be an empty definition. At the same time, even conversational poets like O'Hara, Auden, and Byron, who see their poetic mission as comic and contextual rather than pure, prophetic, and abstract, write in the shadow of the great lyric tradition. Even minor poets (which, by talent or ambition, many of the poets under review declare themselves to be) cannot help but pay indirect homage to the major spirit of Western song as described by Gilbert Murray:

> Love, Strife and Death and that which is beyond Death; an atmosphere formed by the worship of Nature and the enchantment of Memory; a combination of dance and song like the sweep of a great singing bird; all working toward an ecstasy or a transcending of personality, a "standing outside" of the prison of the material present, to be merged in some life that is the object of adoration or desire: these seem to be the subjects, and this the spirit and setting of the primitive MOLPE [dance-and-song] which is the foundation of ancient classical poetry. The tradition, if there is a tradition, rises there.[1]

Thematically, the poems in *Taking Notice*, by Marilyn Hacker, betray their imprisonment in the material present, which Murray suggests it is poetry's archaic mission to escape. Although there is much talk in Hacker about the merging of affectionate bodies and the approach to others as objects of adoration and desire, the poems do not render the transport to which they frequently refer. Neither are they meditations at one remove from the experience; the mood of the volume is one of manic vigilance before the monotony of the present. The most characteristic rhetorical device is the catalogue of highly textured, usually exotic things, arranged in a kind of glossy ad for poetic taste:

> Two blue glasses of neat
> whiskey, epoxy-mended Japanese
> ashtray accruing Marlboro and Gauloise
> butts, umber and Prussian blue ceramic cups
> of Zabar's French Roast, cooling. You acquired
> a paunch; I am almost skinny
> as I'd like to be. You are probably
> right, leaving. We've been here
> thousands of miles away, hundreds of times before.

There is here no beauty that makes the heart yearn (the Greek lyrical ideal), nor is there an active and ample play of consciousness—there is no spiritual truth, there are only things.

The tyranny of objects is marked not only by the prevalence of the catalogue, but also by the propensity of the poet's diction and syntax to clog. "My cleats crunch / the crumble"; "the undulant flat belly / whorled and rose carapaces glimmer under"; "eye-sockets blackberry blotches"; "I fudge a hurt / guess, stir sludge on a page"; "Invoke whatever you can use; / sebaceous pores, querulous gut, / nostalgic genitalia." Syntactically, the effects are also punishing. Intransitive verbs are made transitive: A girl "clambers a bench"; two friends are "leafing magazines for school clothes"; "a pebbled spit" of land is "jutting [present participle] sheer lucidity [object of verb]." Mixed metaphor and misplaced reference are common: "My stomach calms an octave into speech"; "My wrapped sex cups strong drink." Often, the layering of reference leads to statements that are comically obscure: "Serial monogamy is a cogwheeled hurt"; "a spoilt obscenity of choice"; "Apolitical twinges silver through / Nascent blackberry-ripenings." In tone and diction, the poems are both turgid and imprecise.

In another respect, the prosodic, these poems are ill-written. Marilyn Hacker is trying to use stringent stanzaic forms like heroic and tetrameter couplets, quatrains, canzoni, and sonnets; but she has thrown off the fetters of the accentual-syllabic line, counting sometimes stress and sometimes syllables, and sometimes counting both ways in the same poem. Lacking any consistent attitude toward the line, her rhymes become abstract exercises, since the line has not been poised to register and savor them. I quote from the sestet of a sonnet:

> We came for the day
> on a hot bus from Avignon. A Swed-
> ish child hurls a chalk boulder; a tall girl,
> his sister, twelve, tanned, crouches to finger shell-
> whorls bedded in rock-moss. We find our way
> here where we can; we take away what we need.

The chopped-off line breaks are committed with arrogance, not wit. In an accentual-syllabic poem, it is not enough to "count out": The line must also loosely embrace the rhythm it asserts by maintaining a sort of loose territorial unity. Although there is an end-line pause after "a tall girl" in the stanza above, it is a nominal pause inasmuch as the phrase has further—and equivalent—qualifiers, "a tall girl, his sister, twelve, tanned, crouches. . . ." These frequent phrase-bracketings work against any priority of line break over comma. The other line breaks in the stanza are yet more abstract, creating the typographical image of a poetic stanza, but no actual lines of poetry. The obsession with details (the hot bus, Avignon, the chalk boulder, the aspect of the two children, the "shell- / whorls bedded in rock-moss") is peculiarly inward, as if the speaker could not face up to their specificity; so the flat stage props also repel the reader's attention, and the outrageously contrived rhymes (like *Swed-/need*) sound simply amateurish and dispirited.

Marilyn Hacker also writes some rope-dancing poems— the pantoum, the sonnet crown, the sestina, and a poem using only the vowels and *b, c, f, g, h, j, l, n, p, s,* and *y*: "SUN IS SHINING, FINE AS FOIL, / ON AN OCEAN BILGY BLUE.

/ OUCH! I FEEL A FISH AS FLIPPY / AS A FELON FLEE-
ING JAIL." Such poems are tortuous; in no way do they
manage the effortless elation of inspired wordplay—the play
that makes the language feel richer, more daring, more ample
in expressive drive. Instead, under the cloak of play, this
writer masks an undisciplined and unmusical knack with
words. Two stanzas from a sestina illustrate the pointless lip
service paid to formal restraints that, in order to succeed,
ought to seem more accommodating:

> "No good dripping like a bucket from the Well
> of Loneliness, as if there were intrinsic virtue
> in taste or distaste for a harmless act.
> They'll plumb the depths of gloom that they can sink
> to, all unconscious, on the other hand,
> of things they do for which they are account-
>
> able." "You're such a moralist!" the Count-
> ess said. "If I didn't know you so well,
> I never would imagine you could hand-
> le ambiguities so brusquely. Virtue
> is not, speaking abstractly, like that sink-
> ing in melted in chocolate feeling. Act
>
> your age . . .

This is work that practically dares us to find a fault with its
skill, and I find little to mitigate my judgment that the gage is
thrown by poems in which failed irony, dull lists, turgid dic-
tion, and a superficial formalism are artlessly exaggerated.

The other books under review here attempt fewer strin-
gent forms. They exhibit techniques held over from the hey-
day of modernism. All play with the attitudes of surrealism.
William Virgil Davis is a pale copy of Stevens; at their worst,
Gregory Orr and Heather McHugh are latter-day imagists
following William Carlos Williams. Their poems as a group
are afflicted by a stutter, as each proceeds to write the same
knowing poem over and over again: They exaggerate, as it
were, their understatements.

William Virgil Davis is addicted to the portentous declarative sentence. The title poem of *One Way to Reconstruct the Scene* has a characteristic *da capo* structure in which the end rehearses the beginning. The poem is about an automobile accident in winter; I quote the second and final stanzas (three more intervene).

> The girl was thrown free. She lay as if asleep
> against the tree, her hands in her lap.
> Perhaps she was dreaming. The man was still
> behind the wheel, his hand to his head, a cup
> of blood spilled over his yellow shirt. The brake
> pedal was pushed all the way through the floorboard.
> . . . . . . . . . . . . . . . . . . . . . . . . . . . . . . . . . . . . . . . . . . .
> The girl in the blue dress leaned against the tree.
> She seemed to be sleeping. The man remained in the car,
> upright, his blue eyes open. Light snow fell slowly
> through the barren limbs of the tree above the car.
> The moon moved across the sky. It cast a light blue
> reflection on the scene, the snow, the broken glass.

Well-mannered, quaintly overexact ("through the barren limbs of the tree above the car"), stubbornly noncommittal, Davis's style nevertheless has designs on us. We are meant to marvel at his dry-eyed control of material that would (so the posture says) cause softer souls to howl with pity and grief. His poetry, steeled against the entry of emotion, admits only the slightest and most select kinds of rupture, whether the informal savagery of the man's "cup / of blood spilled over his yellow shirt," or the formulaic dash of stylistic color in an otherwise whey-faced descriptive routine.

*The Leaving*

> The light lasted on the window,
> on the sill. The room was already empty,
> abandoned by everything save one gray glove
> fallen, fisted and forgotten,
> by the side of an empty jardinière.
> The wind blew in from the water
> like a landowner. The wagon had been hitched

for hours. The horses stood in the snow
stamping, twitching their ears in the wind.

Except for the unintentionally comic comparison of the lonely
wind to the landowner from central casting, the details have
the brittle vacancy of Robbe-Grillet.

Underlying the grim restraint of Davis's work is perhaps
the belief shared by others writing in the 1960s and 1970s
that pastel versions of the four elements (stone, wind,
moon, pool) have achieved agreed-upon meanings that the
individual poet (not to mention the individual poem) no
longer need defend. As Paul Breslin wrote in *The American
Scholar* three years ago,[2] the contemporary poet's journey to
the interior is sped by mystical cliché. The lexicon of the
new Jungians includes words like "wings, jewels, stones, si-
lence, breath, snow, blood, eats, water, light, bones, roots,
glass, absence, sleep, and darkness. . . . The nouns on this
list," Breslin writes, "have roughly the same status in dis-
course as Jungian archetypes: Their significance is innate
and prior to context." Poets like Davis appear to refer be-
yond these ciphers to a symbolic interior, but it is an inte-
rior without content and without rules. Pain one moment,
glee the next.

Other devices are used to effect the easy transcendence of
the new surrealism. As mentioned earlier, Davis carefully con-
trives the matte finish of a background on which any gesture
or movement, however pale, would look vivid. On this back-
ground the four elements, in their pastel quiescent forms, are
solemnly arranged, and then one of them (to extend Breslin's
analysis a little) is flexed in the direction of action. *Stone* stands
up and walks as *bone*; *pool* turns to *blood*; *moon* scintillates as
*star*; and *wind* arises in the *lungs*, as a *breath*, in a *cry*. The verbs
of endurance (*remember, surround, awaken, sleep, stand, have,
last, fill*) are played against the verbs of aggression (*spit, splin-
ter, dig, eat, shift, take, pull*), often in such a way that passive
verbs and intransitives like *awaken* and *last* and *stand* acquire
the potency of command. Even the use of the article *the*, bland
as it normally is, evokes a sense of prior reference, categorical
existence, and authorial probing:

The bones do not remember the soft skin
surrounding them

they pull the dark blood from the skin
and stand up on their own

they walk in the shapes of shadows
and shine in the dark wind

I've followed them
even though I do not know where they're going

This is poetry both apocalyptic and careless, portentous and coy; I find myself uninterested not only in where the bones are going but also in what they might have been doing there to begin with.

I notice a final surrealist device used by this group of poets, a device perfected by John Ashbery and Mark Strand—the precipitation, from the syntax, of the adverb of tense and duration, often accompanied by tense-shifts in the verb. In Davis's "The Leaving" (quoted above), the adverbs and tense-markers are the source of the second class of poetic inflection performed upon the tangential scenic details (the first inflection being the unlikely, fin-de-siècle diction of "jardinière" and "wind . . . like a landowner"). From this second classification, consider "The room was *already* empty"; "The wagon *had been* hitched *for hours*." The words to watch in the following stanzas from Davis's "Weight Lifter" are *now*, *already*, *ever*, and *long ago*:

Only the weight awaits him. There is nothing
to know. He has only one thing to do. Now,
already, he stands over it, breathing deeply,
then bending, waiting, until, in one instant

of motion, in a blur too quick to be seen, he
lifts it above his head, holds it.
. . . . . . . . . . . . . . . . . . . . . .
If they ever existed, the fields and flowers
faded long ago.

Davis is also using the surrealist technique of mismatching: Unrelated items are thrown together in a vague, impersonal, experiential "field," producing juxtaposition without causal or temporal relation.

Heather McHugh's work approaches generality and cliché from a slightly different direction. Rather than use grammar to precipitate and then to admire the solemn cliché, McHugh uses catchphrase as a "structure" that precipitates the momentary gleam of music, wit, and insight. (God refuses to acknowledge the writers, but after his death, "they would read / themselves into his will.") McHugh is not a profound poet, but she draws interesting effects from her accelerated artifice. The following excerpt, for example, is from a poem that would be ruined by registering more than the slimmest understanding of Berkeley's idealism:

> How could nothing turn so gold?
> You say my eyelid shuts the sky;
> in solid dark I see stars
> as perforations, loneliness
> as blues, what isn't
> as a heavy weight, what is
> as nothing if it's not ephemeral.
>
> ("Message at Sunset for Bishop Berkeley")

However, McHugh has a few bad habits that prevent the poems from moving out of their very small circuits: She becomes formulaic in the middles of poems (the Berkeley poem; "Stall"); she starts to chant "I want" and then assumes that the world conforms to her desire; and finally, she tends to become the most obscure when the poem becomes the most musical: "What summer hasn't shaken / its share of the flourishing / girls from arbors where, aloof, / they could forbear?" But what, one asks, could these allegorical girls forbear to do when *not* shaken from their arbors? Unclear. Yet this excerpt from a poem called "Whoosh" shows a certain gift for a device that none of the other poets so far (except for the negative example of Hacker) uses in any conscious way, and I am speaking of rhyme and its offshoot, alliteration: *shaken/share/flourishing*;

*share/where/forbear.* McHugh is a breath away both from the rhyming quatrain, and from free verse syncopated by rhyme. One model for the euphony McHugh does not entirely catch might be this poem by Julia Randall:

### A Puritan Enters Heaven

I said to my eyes, so far. Harrow
this row. Tomorrow
we shall play hide-and-seek under the grape arbor.

Tomorrow, I said to my ears, we shall sing
how Jack the Journeyman
and the princess in the tower

rhymed as hoofbeats, rode—
I said to my arms and legs,
my arms about her waist,
my lips in her hair—

to a leafy place in the sun
and there, deed done,
white kine without a fence
will watch us dance.[3]

It is obvious that McHugh's is the thinner music. She is not yet sure how to move from the soft middle ground but, since she has an instinct for rising, may yet find her way.

Gregory Orr is a vernacular poet, but rather than verbal cliché, he depends on a strong idiom of association. Consider the reminiscence evoked by a particular angle of field where the speaker had once played hide-and-seek after sundown. Some of the children he sought stood among the horses, but some had climbed the fence and hidden supine in the field, staring up at the stars. It is these, the ones who had entered a realm somehow different from that of the game, whom Gregory Orr the lone seeker is still haunted by.

Now I stand again by the fence
and pluck one rusted strand of wire,
harp of lost worlds. At the sound
the children rise from hiding

and move toward me:
eidolons, adrift on the night air.

("The Lost Children")

I would call to your attention how just are the verb *pluck*, the adjective *rusted*, the metaphor of the *harp*, and the abstraction *eidolons*. Orr has repelled from the poem nothing that was essential to it, unlike William Virgil Davis, who had the air of gritting his teeth to achieve his plainness. "The Lost Children" observes with Edwardian nostalgia the kind of children's limbo we find in early Kafka sketches; it does not falsify its strangeness.

But Gregory Orr does not consistently control his poems. He makes a number of the standard surrealist gestures, nodding now in the direction of Roethke, now in the direction of Mark Strand. One particular flourish that gets in his way is the brilliant but extraneous analogy. (Hayden Carruth has noted this habit in Robert Lowell.) Picking watercress, the speaker's hands become the mouths of dinosaurs "that yank and chew / huge mouthfuls of cress / at the languid delta." By means of such analogies, action in the literal world ceases, stunned, and the poetic neon lights up. What cannot be rendered by plainer recitation is flashed by trope. A boy goes to the barn to feed his three-legged deer.

> "I lived" is the song
> the boy hears as the deer
> hobbles toward him.
> In the barn's huge gloom
> light falls through cracks
> the way swordblades
> pierce a magician's box.

Although the beams of light may look bladelike, and although the barn may then, in some fashion, start to look like a black enamel box, who is the magician? who's the assistant in the box? who is creating the illusion of victimization? who is the accomplice? and (lest one of those swords take off another leg) why hasn't the poem ended "as the deer / hobbles toward him"? Such "literary" analogies are frequently a means to leach significance from moments that perhaps had less than the poet claims, or a somewhat other meaning from the one he is able to remember. Driving home after the funeral of the brother he accidentally shot, the speaker of another poem plays on our sympathies as he frames grotesques: "In the dark, a wadded / kleenex his mother pressed / against her cheek / was a white snail / eating holes in a leaf." Some experiences cannot be absorbed, let alone made into art. Orr is sideswiping here, presuming on our ready pity to excuse silly writing.

When not put off by fakery and by merely flubbed writing, I can find things to like about all these poets. However, I seem to have serious doubts about the literary maturity of any one of them. I grouped them together because each repeats him/ herself to a fault, has a relatively monotonic voice, and makes many of the same redundant gestures of "knowing" that the others make. Above all, none of these writers, felicitous or not, offers us a poetry whose spirit or form lays hold of the imagination. Even the nice moments and attractive lines and appropriate perceptions too readily fade from the mind. Hence the title of this essay. The generation of silver, you recall, was golden neither in body nor in spirit.

> A child was brought up at his good mother's side an hundred years, an utter simpleton, playing childishly in his own home. But when they were full grown and were come to the full measure of their prime, they lived only a little time and that in sorrow because of their foolishness.[4]

The next pair of books exhibit more care for continuity and perhaps more sheer hard work. But since they use lineation either according to private whim or mere numerical bracketing, both are in prose. James McMichael's *Four Good Things* is the most arduous—a plain-style lyric of self-conscious diffidence extrapolated to fill seventy pages of continuous text. It is written in a blank verse so extruded as to be indistinguishable as a meter. At first, I thought that the principle of selection for the themes and movements in these two-thousand lines was the imposition of order upon trivia. But McMichael does not wish to sort his world this way, even if one of the central metaphors of the work puts autobiography into play as the only reliable map of the world that has been touched by the perceiving subject.

Memory's map apportions to the speaker's father, a real estate broker in Pasadena, the perimeters and elliptical character of that city. During his wife's long illness (which the son believes began at his conception), the father works later and longer hours; in the father's absence, the boy examines his task for the first time. He must, to remain in connection with his parent, imagine where his father might be. "He would be somewhere within his maps at any time." People matter only to the extent that his father needs them to do business with. About both places and persons, father and son are alike indifferent: "Where they were, / what they cared about or did was less insistent / than the fact that they were there at any time for him. / They were his continuity as he was mine." Not only is this poorly written, it is indulgent toward the very arbitrariness its style exposes to view. McMichael tries to bring everything he describes down to the level of *this-and-that*. He tries to locate himself on the map of other people's meanings, but always by way of this selective depopulation that he and his father practice, whereby neighborhood is defined as the blur one's own alienation imposes: "The vagueness of the city when I looked at it / was my exclusion from the lives that made it clear."

While McMichael cares little for people, he cares sentimentally for his categories for them (fear being another form of this sentiment). He recoils in fascination from schemes of number and average (and here the urban statisticians join hands with Big Brother—the founders of the British mills and the California scientific combines, Aerojet, Cal Tech, and Mt. Palomar); the computer, the dynamo, and the cathode ray tube threaten the speaker's anonymity with their own.

> Because it remembers
> perfectly, because it never sleeps, because it can
> sort and compare and choose and find the proper

order in the sum of all its pulses, ON or OFF,
the things they say in eighteen million homes are
digitized and stored, revised, called up again by
GEOCODE with its coordinates for any point
P on the map, all references on grid and bearing
east and west in equal squares from their false origin.
We're somewhere in its mesh of cells and always
catching up.

Whether caught in the mesh of computer cells or left entirely out of the picture by distorting cartographers, McMichael eventually proves that he has no use for other people's maps.

What McMichael substitutes is a stylistically closed system where he can play God. He need not identify any *it* or *what* that might crop up in a sentence about knowledge or perception. He can diddle abstractions like *possibility* and *sense*. He can turn the whole syntax on the adverbs *how*, *only*, *much*, *never*, and *almost*, the indefinites *some*, *most*, *other*, *any*, and the crucial conjunction for such a dry and empty style, *or*. These are further devices of the style of *this-and-that*, smug, solipsistic, vague, full of hopped-up intensities that do not focus on anything, and, in its flattest and least focused moments, totally banal: "Each minor thing they cared about / earned what it had to do with matters that were / not their business." One notes the cant term *earned*, which, like *risk*, *danger*, and *forgiveness*, is too often in contemporary poetry postulated of the mere act of connecting *A* to *B* in the field of ordinary vision. The same sort of doom attends our dealings with people.

Whether describing a mentally disturbed boy, a sexual encounter, the retired couples who come to California to die, or the testing of wind-drag on an aircraft, McMichael makes the world sound like a collection of consciousnesses that practice automatic writing. Even the arroyo has its bland recitation; even the houses, after the author finishes denuding them of people, are boringly insomniac. The rhapsodies of detail in which the speaker periodically indulges, for all their particular inclusiveness, serve the purpose of purification from the human. Once scoured, the places receive a little child's idea of significant form: "My longing for it now enclosed it in my not / being there to let it get away."

Alicia Ostriker's *Mother/Child Papers* describes, first, the birth and nurture of the author's third child. Second, the book falls under the demonic shadow of the 1970 invasion of Cambodia and the 1975 evacuation of Phnom Penh. But on the third and most telling view, Ostriker's work details the achievement of a connection between personal history and public fact as both present themselves to a very intelligent and interesting writer.

The first half of *The Mother/Child Papers* is an indictment of the deceit of politicians and obstetricians. Nixon had "wanted his own war" ("'This is not an invasion'") just as the doctor had wanted his own way in the labor and delivery of his patient. The author was given a spinal block she did not want or need, which prevented her from doing what she had planned to do to get her third child born. "I am conscious, only my joy is cut off. I feel the stainless will of everyone." Further on we read of the guardsmen's bayonets at Kent State and the postpartum "swordlike headaches" from the spinal anaesthetic—an odd juxtaposition that nevertheless glows with insight, as if Ostriker's child were Balder the Beautiful and Ostriker herself the goddess Frigg helpless to shield him from Loki. I bring up the myth because good literature is allusive—archetypal—in the way it embodies our humanity. Put another way, the Norse myth itself embodies the profound tactile and hormonal connection between newborn and mother, a connection that, instead of shutting the world out, solicits its aid and admiration against incomprehensible threats. At the child Gabriel's delivery,

> the father is blushing, he notices how the genitals
> nod and bob, ornamental and puffy, mushrooms and
>     ladyslipper,
> do you hear this fellow yell now, smiles the doctor, he'll be a
>     soldier.
>
> They have wiped the flesh, it becomes a package, they wheel
>     it away, clean
> and alone, the mother rests on a plump pillow and is weeping

in the pretty room, her breasts are engorged, she is filling
    with desire,
she has thrown a newspaper to the floor, her television is
    dark, her
intention is to possess this baby, this piece of earth, not to
    surrender
a boy to the ring of killers. They bring him, crying. Her
    throat leaps.

                                      ("Mother/Child")

Nothing in the novels of Margaret Drabble is as affecting, as
convincing, as these few lines of Ostriker's. But then, Drab-
ble's world is comparatively self-enclosed, and marred by the
suspicion that Drabble is playing to the male characters who
happen to find lactation placidly erotic. There is no sense in
Ostriker's book that she is playing, or playing to, anyone.
When she talks about her family, she refrains from clouding
their beings with unexamined feeling. These four people who
make up the author's domestic world are neither indulged
nor overridden by her portrayals of them.

    Among many lineated writings, Ostriker has produced
two fine poems, "The Change" and "In the Dust," both
about the difficult truce between a mother and the world to
which she must relinquish her older daughter, especially
since the girl has begun to burn with her own perfection and
her own restlessness.

What is that whirling in the dust?
What is that powerful
movement, everywhere, so rapid she cannot see it?
The fireflies are making their phosphorous, slow circles,
the appletrees ripening, and she
is going willingly. I send her willingly.

                                       ("In the Dust")

The lineation here creates at least two effects a prose version
would not. It separates *powerful* from *movement*, brightening
the adjective and dimming the noun to a haunting, persistent
humming. And in the penultimate line, lineation suspends the
breath after *she*, who is not only the daughter who is the subject

of the poem, but also a verbal magnet to the stanza's near rhymes, *see*, *making*, *ripening*, *going*, and *willingly*. Perhaps Ostriker would be uncomfortable with the sheer density of feeling if her stanza were to be printed as prose. But the virtues of good prose (continuity, well-orchestrated eloquence, and strong predication) are not all that move me to recommend the book.

## NOTES

1. Gilbert Murray, *The Classical Tradition in Poetry* (1927), quoted by Louise Bogan in her essay "The Pleasures of Formal Poetry" (1953), which is collected in her *Poet's Alphabet: Reflections on the Literary Art and Vocation*, ed. Robert Phelps and Ruth Limmer (New York: McGraw-Hill, 1970), p. 154.

2. Paul Breslin, "How to Read the New Contemporary Poem," *American Scholar* (Summer 1978).

3. Julia Randall, *The Farewells* (Chicago: Elpenor Books, 1981).

4. Hesiod, *Works and Days*, trans. H. G. Evelyn-White, in W. H. Auden, ed., *The Portable Greek Reader* (New York: Viking, 1948), p. 56.

# Biological Passion Play

Bruno Bettelheim tells a haunting anecdote about an autistic child so repelled by people that she was difficult not only to reach on a human level but even to feed. He describes how she "prowled" at night, approachable only by her favorite counselor, who "roamed through the building with her for many hours each night, feeding her as they went" (*The Empty Fortress*, 1967). This is the kind of night ramble that would appeal to the poet Donald Finkel; it is a scene of dull terror on the part of the afflicted child, of an almost impersonal charity on the part of the counselor and, on the simplest level, of enormous tactical and rhythmic aggravations as the one tries to feed the other.

Bettelheim uses this anecdote to suggest how easy it is to misconstrue wild autism as literal ferality, hence how difficult it is to disprove myths about so-called "wolf children." But for the bard and the storyteller—for a writer like Finkel—what would be fascinating is the reality of those nights: the hours of wearisome pacing through the halls and the common rooms of the clinic; the counselor's efforts to continue speaking in a direct and affectionate way despite the little girl's recoil from contact, her self-absorption, her nudity, her matted hair, her smell, her bared teeth . . . and there is something else. I suspect that most artists would be appalled—and obsessed—by an idea hardly hinted at by Bettelheim: the idea that the distance between watcher and watched is the work of an instant to bridge.

---

Review of Donald Finkel, *What Manner of Beast* (New York: Atheneum, 1981).

Most artists would, I think, view these two characters as parts of the same self.

Of course, this aesthetic identification is not one that will help cure the autistic, nor will it necessarily reduce the amount of evil in the world by increasing the amount of sympathy. It is not even a literal assumption about the ego. It is an instantaneous and, if you will, archetypal "leap" by which the artist might seek to hold in one instant—in one figure—the disparate and eccentric antagonisms of our nature.

Finkel's most compelling metaphors for the conflicts between one state of being and another involve the idea of suspension in different mediums. An Indian encountered on Martin Frobisher's first Arctic voyage in 1576 is said to approach objects with a fanciful awe; he strokes, raps, and rubs the furniture instead of sitting down on it. In the Indian's iconic medium, spectacles are "wafers of moon / frozen so fast they will not come / unfrozen, even on his tongue." Despite the lyricism and the restraint of these descriptions, Finkel is portraying a strangeness that is both disturbing and aggressive; something in our modesty is subtly outraged when the Indian "touches his tongue to the lens of the Master's glass."

*What Manner of Beast* is a suite of poems about the fearful ease of permeating the boundary between the human realm and the merely animal. It has a dual subject: the "humanity" (that is, the shared intelligence, the need for affection, and the ability to "play") of primitives and lesser animals, and the "animality" (the shared bewilderment, the darkness, the resort to instinct) of modern men and women. Owing to the correspondence between these two realms, every cruel act by a beast (for example, rival apes tearing each other's infants to bits) is matched with equally gratuitous acts committed by men (by tribesmen in Zaire, by supposedly friendly Chipewyans in Canada). Finkel then takes the analogy further so that, for every dark intention within primitive men alluded to in his sources, he excerpts yet more chilling and indefensible motives on the part of men presumed civilized (the voyages of Frobisher and Richard Hakluyt abound in examples). Finally, lest sixteenth-century "civilization" seem a bit rough and ready, Finkel in other poems gives us contemporary examples, bringing in a horde of scientists and technicians as evidence of the limited sympathy evinced by "advanced" investigators of nonhuman behavior.

Many of these behavioral biologists are trying to teach primates to master sign languages, to deal in abstractions, to postpone gratification, and to adopt symbolic tokens (hence, to use money), but these are lessons inculcated at great cost. Other animals are used as bribes, withheld if the subject animals fail to pay attention or learn quickly enough. All the animals are caged. All are sexually deprived. All are constantly watched. And in Finkel's laboratory the chimpanzee Lana must face an authority figure more powerful and more vulgar than Arthur Koestler's commissar: "[B]etween the hunger and the monkey chow / lies the machine / between the boredom and the colored slides / the machine, which once / toward morning, she entreated / *Please tickle Lana*" ("The Beast in the Machine"). The machine is indeed a cruel tutor, the more so when it can subdue its own inventors, like Finkel's persona, the graduate student "Roger," whom the learning machine has also trapped: "My clipboard calls like a siren." Roger and the chimpanzee Lucy are like lovers lost in a forest of word-match tab and wingèd clockface:

> *hurry*, she signs to me
> fluttering those ecstatic hands
> while from under the clip the seconds
> trickle from my side like rills of blood
>
> ("Chase Lucy")

> at my back, the kettle's keening litanies
> the seconds scuttle through my Timex crystal
> like fugitives, while under my pen
> the word-list whispers, *listen*
>
> ("That Listen")

Finkel's poetic method has been likened to collage—the interleaving of found, quoted, and overheard material with his own dramatic, unpunctuated free verse, in which the space at the end of the line often does double duty: It sometimes implies a period and other times a run-on to the next line. The poet also uses multiple voices distinguished by italics and indentation, as in the eerie "gospels" of the Emperor penguins in his superb *Adequate Earth* (1972) or in the songs of the captured Eskimos in the present volume. Finkel is uncannily deft at finding eloquent and credible language for the speechless and the alien—again, by virtue of extraordinary leaps of insight.

The more daring of these intuitive leaps occur in the erotic poems. I should caution readers that Finkel comes from the same school of hysterical sexual description as do the prose writers Robert Coover, Stanley Elkin, and Philip Roth. From Finkel's earlier books: "My groin clangs like a shovel on a stone"; "screwing dizzily / into her unctuous socket"; the poet searches for "a climax lasting days"; "I flowed / down her shadowy snatch." Five of Finkel's volumes have been marred by this sort of strip-joint surrealism. But increasingly since *The Garbage Wars* in 1970, Finkel has chosen to incorporate his peculiar blend of ego and prophecy in less self-flattering ways. Thus when he describes the ingenious wooing of the dolphin Peter and the shadowy arousal of the woman (Margaret Howe) who has been trying to teach the animal to say her name, Finkel is commenting on the ludicrous aspects of the relationship without relinquishing the poignant ones. The poem is called "MMMMMM":

> her ankles sting from the nicks of his teeth
> · · · · · · · · · · · · · · · · · · · · · · · · · · · · · · · · ·
> playing, he lets his favorite ball
> roll back in his mouth, parting his teeth
> in a permanent smile, as if to say
> *Come I won't hurt you*
>
> > *I stand very still, legs slightly apart, and Peter slides his mouth*
> > *gently over my shin. His mouth opens all the way and he begins*
> > *up and down my leg. Then the other leg.*
>
> a month of this salty courtship
> till one evening, in the second moon
> of their togethering, he lets the ball
> slip from his mouth entirely

```
and, rolling on his side
approaches
MARGARET:     MMMMMM
MMAGRIT Yes!
Yes! (clapping)
That's
PETER: (softly) Mxx xxx
MARGARET: an EM. Say . . .
    MMAGRIT
PETER: mxxxxxxxxx
```

Margaret's rhetoric is both banal and pornographic ("I am completely vulnerable to him"), and of course Finkel's stage-whisper primitivism is grating ("second moon," "together"), but like all the romances in *What Manner of Beast*, the urgent meetings between Peter and Margaret are hopelessly false; lacking any proper language, they must fall back on laboratory cliché—while, even as cliché is reinvoked, the poem registers the shudder of threatened taboo.

Even when his subject is the baffled puberty of the wild child found in France in the late eighteenth century, Finkel shows by his subtle stylistic parody that not even the cult of sensibility can mask the housekeeper's dullness of vision or the doctor's hardness of heart. Madame Guerin is indirectly explaining why, early each Sunday morning, Victor can be heard calling out "*lli lli lli*"; the doctor's analysis appears in italics:

> how many Sundays was it, Julie
> had joined them for dinner? her faultless Julie
> of the downcast eyes, the forthright breasts
> that could impale a saint, provoke
> not a sound, but a psalm of longing
> a song such as infant Solomon
> might croon in his cradle, *Julie*
>
> > *I have seen him in a company of women attempting to relieve his*
> > *uneasiness by sitting beside one of them and gently taking hold of*
> > *her hand, her arms and her knees*

When he died at forty-three, Victor was celibate. Madame Guerin had remained with him, powerless to help let alone understand him, but nevertheless stricken by his loneliness. The poem ends with her silent keening (as Victor has cried aloud for *lli lli lli*), the cry "like a fishbone caught in her throat / *Victor*."

Like many of the transfers of sympathy in Finkel's new book, Madame Guerin's mourning is both involuntary and enormously affecting. Although none of the characters in the book's loosely constructed biological passion play is particularly heroic or majestic, the poet makes the agon in which each is engaged seem momentous. In one of the many slighter poems that float about the larger ones like small pilot fish, Donald Finkel speaks through a young tuna fisherman who had only one way to free the dolphin he had caught by accident:

> the wicked moonlight
> winks at the tip of my grappling hook
> as I plunge it into the frantic fabric
> it's only the work of an instant
> to free her
>
> and lightyears before
> I lose sight of her
> sinking among gull-scraps
> wearing the old imperturbable smile
> unresisting, a goddess of garbage
> the word made meat

The dead mammal with the mermaid smile sinks into the slough of memory, the endless casualty of another night ramble with cool imperturbable art.

# From "Collected and Selected"

The British poet Frank Templeton Prince (b. 1912) is best known in this country to students of late Renaissance literature for his excellent study of the origins of Milton's diction and rhythms, *The Italian Element in Milton's Verse* (1954).[1] But he is also, like Empson and Winters, a very fine academic poet, which is to say, one whose scholarship outweighs, in merit and in bulk, his poems, and whose tendency is to load the poetic work with learning, both historical and metrical, making it almost involuntarily didactic. Prince's historical portraits, from "Words from Edmund Burke" in 1938 to the Laurence Sterne pastiche that closes the *Collected Poems* (1979), are generally overburdened by their own accuracy.

In his twenty-page "Drypoints of the Hasidim" (1975), however, the scholarly punctilio exists to serve a vision beyond mere mastery over detail. Here the poet is haunted by the paradox of the Eastern European Hasidic movement (roughly 1750 to 1800)—namely, that the plain man's illumination counted for more than either the Rabbi's specialized learning or the mystic's closed code, that the community of plain Jews in exile *was* Israel, miracle, and the purpose of the world, and yet that, when you looked closely, there was only separation, oblivion, loneliness, "And moonlight silvering wooden walls / And

Review of F. T. Prince, *Collected Poems* (New York: Sheep Meadow Press, 1973); Lawrence Durrell, *Collected Poems 1931–1974* (New York: Viking, 1980); Laura (Riding) Jackson, *The Poems of Laura Riding* (New York: Persea Books, 1980); Daryl Hine, *Selected Poems* (New York: Atheneum, 1981); Janet Lewis, *Poems Old and New 1918– 1978* (Athens, Ohio: Swallow Press, 1981).

greasy alleys and the market square / Left empty but for litter."
Hasidism (piety) had its own melancholy built into it, for even
as the common man was praised, he was dissolved to nothing in
parabolic distinctions left over from rabbinical habit.

The great monument to Hasidism is the collection of saints'
lives, parables about the Polish and Russian Maggids (Mas-
ters), in which, after a time, the telling of the story became
more important than the message of the story itself. A literary
self-consciousness began to function of itself, emphasizing not
only the distance between the teller and the subject, but also
the frail, flamelike tissue of the remnant of language from
which the story was cut. Systems of belief that turn from com-
munal dogma to the individual soul tend to break on the issue
of psychological reality (gnostic Christianity experienced the
same institutional weakening). Leadership splinters. If any-
one can be Messiah, the center of meaning, then no one can
certainly be Messiah in the sentimental, practical, chiliastic
sense:

> Rays, glimpses in shadow
>                         and that sweetness—
> Love justice sonship brotherhood—
> Which makes the longing of the world:
>                         Messiah son of Joseph
> Who could be anywhere
>                         a youth half-grown
>                 Born anywhere in Hungary or Poland
>
>                 —Perhaps the boy of seventeen
> Who had undoubtedly been seen
>                 In Buda, with a threadbare coat
>
> And a face of amazing starlike purity

"Drypoints of the Hasidim" is composed of twenty-two sec-
tions of what might be called free-verse "fields," in which
liquid rhythms, strong indentations, interior rhymes, and jux-
taposition are the main prosodic means. The rhetoric of each
"field" narrows itself to a trope of illumination-by-fade-out, as
in the parable, where the last remark is shockingly insufficient
to the foregoing matter and thereby inversely resonant. This

method highlights one brief insight against a background that is already dimming and half-mythical, as in the Messiah passage quoted above, or in the poem's opening section, at the end of which we follow the journey of the East European elect, forced to pursue low trades and rough lives,

> Riding and plodding on bad roads
> By valleys in the dark Carpathians
> >           threaded with tawny crystal
> Past battered cottages and farms
> With yellow middens and a dog in chains,
> >     And osiers by a stream

One feels that the chained dog evokes from the wanderer a personal pang, and that the veins of tawny crystal and the willow wands stem from a talent for perception both fleeting and poisonous in its gift of loveliness.

As for the natural beauties, so for the spiritual ones (those hopes that attach to faces of a starlike purity; those sparks in inanimate things drawn forth to shine in men of God): They are intuitions that consume themselves in their own articulation, just as the eighteenth- and nineteenth-century Hasidim were obscured by the records that grew up about them, and, finally, just as the "drypoint" engraving process alluded to in Prince's title vitiates itself after a very few printings. The poem thus engages its energies on a number of fronts at once. It has to do with people, a period, a local religious movement, a way of telling in parable, and with a process of plastic creation that is perforce ephemeral—all of these topics shadowing the others, and outlining as well the poet's idea of the imagination, whose light is constant, only not in this world.

"Drypoints of the Hasidim" is a fine example of deeply drawn intellectual pathos. So is "Soldiers Bathing," the title poem of Prince's 1954 volume. The structure of the elegiac couplets is complex, but the narrative structure is simple enough. We move from the present scene to an aesthetic meditation and back to the present scene. But the intermediate matter of the poem is more than cultivated free association with a couple of Florentine artworks. It is evening in wartime.

The speaker's troops are bathing naked and become more beautiful and less bestial out of their clothes. The scene reminds the speaker of a drawing by Michelangelo of soldiers surprised by the enemy and buckling their weapons over their still naked flesh (thus suggesting that the present interlude is not without its threat of interruption). Then he is reminded of a yet more violent work, a painting by Pollaiuolo of brutal man-to-man engagements between naked warriors against a "sinister red ground,"

> Beneath a sky where even the air flows
> With *lachrimae Christi*. For that rage, that bitterness, those
>      blows
> That hatred of the slain, what could they be
> But indirectly or directly a commentary
> On the Crucifixion? And the picture burns
> With indignation and pity and despair by turns,
> Because it is the obverse of the scene
> Where Christ hangs murdered, stripped, upon the Cross. I
>      mean,
> That is the explanation of its rage.

Like the painter, the speaker views war through the lens of an act that was designed to end wars. To anticipate a bit, Prince closes the poem, after returning to his men bathing, with a streak of red in the Western sky "that might have issued from Christ's breast." If this were the only connection the poem made, the irony would be patent, and too easily come by: We are still living on the wrong side of the canvas; at best, in our thick-necked way, we can perceive the good by its opposite.

But that is not quite how "Soldiers Bathing" is argued. Between the explanation of the painting's rage and the streak from Christ's breast, there occurs a more demanding claim, one that would not have been unusual in the seventeenth century but is quite startling in the twentieth. We war because the love of Christ is frightening; "we prefer the freedom of our crimes" to the servitude implied by a shadow world.

> . . . some great love is over all we do,
> And that is what has driven us to this fury, for so few

Can suffer all the terror of that love:
The terror of that love has set us spinning in this groove
Greased with our blood.

The world is Christ's *oeuvre au noir*, the bleakest reduction before the transmutation of the flesh. The small freshenings of the body in "Soldiers Bathing" occur in the foreground against these violent exhalations from the shadow world, which eventually becomes the only real one.

In the third of Prince's poems I will touch on, narrative distortion is at its most extreme. One could say that "Apollo and the Sibyl" (1954) is "about" memory reflecting on the losses of youth, affection, adventure, wholeness, and that the mythic figures are suspended over the extraordinarily beautiful, Eliot-like free verse only to suggest a nobility in the expanse of the feeling. In other words, one could read "Apollo and the Sibyl" as a love poem magnified by regret:

I remain in my pain that is
A golden distance endlessly,
And with my head bent, and my eyes
That follow down and stare
As with a dreaming stare, I gaze
Until the noon that climbs the air
Troubles, makes more than ever now excessive
—Rubbed and ruffled, thumbed—
Outrageously more beautiful,
The burning young tumescent sea,

And the smoke-black stone-pine, wings wide on the hushed
    air,
Hangs over its own shadow, tilted:
Smouldering incense of the pine,
Under the noonday, over the dark pool, cool.

            —And the sky opens
Like a fan its vault of violet light, unfolding
A wide and wingless path to the impossible.

These verses portray both self-absorption (the bent head, the pine brooding over its own shadow) and possession by the Other (the pine symbolizes this possession as well, whether viewed as another vessel like the speaker, stock-still in anticipation, or as a vehicle of descent whose "wings" are "wide"). The vault of light opening into "the impossible" then suggests a double relation between itself and the speaker, whether within herself is amplified this painful arena of the past, or whether, beyond herself, the whole sky of memory opens, forcing her to witness the magnitudes of her loss.

This "local" reading of the ominous lines that close the 240-line "Apollo and the Sibyl" makes perfect sense, but if applied to all the other long passages of landscape-brooding, will be found insufficient to keep the poem from cloying:

> The air is stirring, everywhere
> A sweetness dignifies the air:
> The broom, that tanned and dusty angel,
> Bound down, is taken by the hair
> And rifled, and blown lingeringly, or plunged
> By the wind's tooth and talon, torn
> But living and enduring . . .
> . . . . . . . . . . . . . . . . . . . . . . .
> —Burning and ribbed abysses, broken cradles, empty shores
> And the uneasy airy glitter, the slow glow
> And then the massive flash
> That answers irresistibly,
> And sobs and rubs and woos,
> Mirrors and writhes and rocks itself and sighs
> And strives to glut itself with light . . .

In a realistic reading of the first passage, the woman identifies herself with the dry and helpless broom flower, blown hither and yon at the will of the weather—at best, a sentimental self-portrait by an old woman unable to control the drift of her thoughts. In the second passage, psychological realism would have the speaker distorting the violent action of the Mediterranean light by virtue of some sudden access of turmoil in herself.

Both interpretations would be banal. Nor would either reading quite account for the facts we are given. The first passage above continues: ". . . torn / But living and enduring, the sweet doom / Like an imaginary face / Springs out of the rough shrub and floats in ambush, / To honey our disgrace." Prince has found a frame for the otherwise violent pathetic fallacy of Romantic landscape description. Similarly in the second passage, in which a "slow glow" is followed by a "massive flash" of light, the poet registers the ancient and unpsychological theme of the poem, that Apollo is light, in his calm moods caressing shapes and stretching glinting shields over water, in moments of access piercing the prophetess with lightning.

Vergil says that when Aeneas and his men come to Cumae, the Sibyl twice attempts to resist the invasion of the god who held a goad to her brain. Until she submits, she runs madly through her cave,

> as if in hope of casting the God's power from her brain. Yet all the more did he torment her frantic countenance, overmastering her wild thoughts, and crushed her and shaped her to his will. So at last, of their own accord, the hundred tremendous orifices in the shrine swung open, and they carried through the air the answer which the prophetess gave. . . . [2]

The crushing of the little broom flower in Prince's poem represents precisely the unwilled religious possession Vergil describes, just as the obedience of the rocks to the call of the god (in Prince's phrases, "broken cradles, empty shores") mirrors the readiness of the hollow tunnels in the *Aeneid* to amplify the maid's voice; all matter is responsive to Apollo.

Prince's "Apollo and the Sibyl" is thus more than a love poem, it is the record of a life-long punishment partially welcomed by the Sibyl, who remained a virgin somewhat confused by the intuition of what she had rejected. The sun-bathed Mediterranean world is drawn by Prince as a place of violent beauty and utter loneliness, in which the Sybil's life is an agony of longing toward a tyrannic presence who will neither release her nor allow himself to be seen: "—And the sky opens / Like a fan its vault of violet light, unfolding / A wide and wingless path to the impossible."

As I search for refined terms in which to pay my final compliments to the poems of F. T. Prince, I realize that the three poems about which I have spoken touch the three major sources of the Western imagination, Hebraic, Christian, and Greco-Roman apotheosis. "Chaka" (1938), a superior suite of poems spoken by a native king of the Sudan, only enlarges the range of his imaginative achievement. I am delighted that the Sheep Meadow Press has brought out an attractive and inexpensive paperback so that more Americans might profit from this overlooked master.

What strikes me first about the poetry of Lawrence Durrell is its ventriloquism. The tetrameters of Durrell's "Prayer-Wheel" (1940) at times echo part 2 of Eliot's "Burnt Norton" (1936), at others Auden's "Lullaby" (1939). Durrell's early love poems have affinities with the turn-of-mind and the local rhetoric of Yeats, especially in the use of the interrogative followed by an emphatic "No!" and in the homely language of his self-deprecation: "[C]an the mind / Transliterate such metamorphosis / Evoking thence / More than a leaning pothook for a sense?" (Durrell, "Love Poems," iii, 1934). A different kind of intensity, which reifies images and mixes metaphors, links Durrell's work to Dylan Thomas's:

> . . . At Funchal the blackish yeast
> Of the winter sea I hated rubbed
> And gobbled on a thousand capes
> . . . . . . . . . . . . . . . . . . . . . . . . . . .
> . . . the water coiled backwards
> Like a spring to press its tides
> Idle and uniform as grapes in presses
> Descrying a horizontal mood,
> The weather slowing like a pedal . . .
>
> (Durrell, "Funchal," 1948)

> Who kills my history?
> The year-hedged row is lame with flint,
> Blunt scythe and waterblade.
> . . . . . . . . . . . . . . . . . . . . . . .
> Who in these labyrinths,
> The tidethread and the lane of scales,
> Twine in a moon-blown shell,
> Escape to the flat cities' sails . . . ?
>
> (Thomas, "Then Was My Neophyte," 1936)

Lawrence Durrell is more realistic than Thomas, more Shakespearean than Yeats, more cabalistic than Auden, and more declarative than Eliot; and yet the resemblances to these four writers, and many more, haunt the *Collected Poems* of Durrell, who from the start of his career has carried on what looks like a double apprenticeship, both to the poetic tradition, and to Mediterranean place-feeling, without ever becoming settled in any one tone or form. His poems sound as episodic as his novels, and as readers of both know, many of his poems are clearer once you have read *Justine* (1957), just as the novels re-weave many of the workbook notes that were first published as poems.

In addition to their debt to the four poets above, both the *Alexandria Quartet* and Durrell's poetry invoke the spirit of the "old man" of Alexandria, the Greek poet Konstantin Kavafis (1863–1933), whom Durrell (b. 1912) invests with the same kind of uncanny ubiquitousness with which Latin American writers like García Márquez and Sábato invest Borges. The brief, bittersweet love affair, a constant theme in the personal poems of Kavafis, was so intimately bound up with the city—the cafés, the shops, the rented rooms—that Durrell could find in Kavafis a warrant for his own temperamental nostalgia, just as he found in the Alexandria of the old poet a complex symbol for exile, placelessness, and cultural deterioration. The symbolism is made more poignant for the heterosexual Durrell by Kavafis's homosexuality.

But there are yet more important differences between them. Not only did Kavafis devote two-thirds of his oeuvre to obscure historical voices from the Levant: His poems are also exclusively dramatic. Description enters as a measure of and grounding for character. In Durrell, technicalities of place overshadow character and response. Furthermore, as Auden noted, Kavafis uses few local tropes, almost no similes or metaphors. The major "trope" in Kavafis is always temporal juxtaposition; "then" plays against "now," and in that play the dramatic memories rise to their point. In Kavafis's most famous poem, "The City" (written 1894), the streets and neighborhoods are literal. In the loose rendering Durrell put at the end of the novel *Justine*, they become metaphoric, "mental suburbs" and "earthly landfalls."

Whereas Durrell in his poems writes about history, often abstractly, Kavafis wrote from within history, obtaining immediacy from understatement. In one of Durrell's best historical poems, "On First Looking into Loeb's Horace," the Latin poet remains distant, perhaps a kindred spirit, but lodged in the trope of nostalgia, which is to say, in the poet's own fascination with the faraway. Durrell makes the city of Athens at once pastel and Babylonian, and burned-out:

> Footloose on the inclining earth
> The long ships moved through cities
> Made of loaf-sugar, tamed by gardens,
> Lying hanging by the hair within the waters
> . . . . . . . . . . . . . . . . . . . . . . . . . . . . . . . . . . .
> Chapters of clay and whitewash. Others here
> Find only a jar of red clay, a Pan
> The superstitious whipped and overturned.
> Yet nothing of ourselves can equal it
>
> Though grown from causes we still share,
> The natural lovely order, as where water
> Touches earth, a tree grows up . . .
>
> ("The Parthenon," 1945)

The visual stillness and self-containedness of the Greek world are well rendered, as is the breach we create by a disbelief that confronts the same data as "they" did, but without the same accommodation to it. Thus the historical grows awkward and quaint.

This sense of our severance from our own beginnings is one of the main themes of Durrell's poetry. On page after page, he worries the theme with the same rhetorical gestures: First, with a kind of puzzled absorption, he arranges the descriptive pieces, and when he finds them lifeless or merely evocative, he will, to quote Cyril Connolly on Durrell's friend Henry Miller, "go into overdrive like a car." At last, to end the poem, the poet will cast about for some sad, contingent solution (like Matthew Arnold):

Permutations of a rose, buried beneath us now,
Under the skin of thinking like a gland
Discharging its obligations in something trivial:
Say a kiss, a handclasp: say a stone tear.

("In Rhodes," 1948)

The gland that discharges in the pitiful stone tear is a mental/sexual organ of which Durrell is the lone anatomist. Such vocabulary is a product of the "overdrive" that in other poems will tear the black fig of Desire from the belly of Reason, or present the dreams of men obliterated "by colder coitus in the mind of God." A young prostitute beds an old philosopher in order to be "bathed in the spray of his sperm / The pneuma of his inner idea." Lovers contract "the sempiternal clap." To read is to "finger the sex of many an uncut book." Da Vinci is said to be touched by "time's fragility, the semen of fate." An artist "deflower[s] the secret contours of a mind"—a metaphor that, like many of those just quoted, is intelligible only if not considered too closely. At its most naked, Durrell's sexual bullying exposes members in every landscape: Greece is "the vexed clitoris of the continental body." Why Greece should not be the vexed phallus, we must leave to the womanizer to explain, for woman is a "crucifixion on the Word. / We press on her as Roman on his sword." The color of a woman's lips is "pink as the sex of a mastiff." And nothing can mask the smug misogyny of the long "Elegy on the Closing of the French Brothels" (1947).

Related to Durrell's sexual mysteries is the idea of words and the Word as keys to the things they name. He sees the world, even the world of sex, in linguistic terms. Alluding to his version of gnostic initiation and betrayal, Durrell says that "sex became / A lesser sort of speech, and the members doors." The moments after lovemaking reverberate with "a dying language / Of perfume." Lovers speak a "huge glossary / Of whispers." The ocean speaks in vowels. Roses on a hill form a "vocabulary." The poet keeps reading the "same lexicon, stars over water." And Durrell's poem "Bere Regis" surveys English poetry in terms of the grammar of the English landscape, the "expurgated prose-land" of winter, the "Moss walls, woolen forests," and "mnemonic valley" where "the thrush familiarises" and over the rural cote rises "a colloquial moon." A more twisted logic makes love "the grammar of that war / Which time's the only *ointment* for" (my emphasis).

I mention both of Durrell's subtexts, the gnostic/profane and the language of the earth, because they are so frequently the switches he throws when he wants to go into overdrive. Durrell is forever pushing buttons, starting old arguments with himself, and leaping erratically from description to diatribe, from pretty view to a collision of metaphors. On the other hand, anyone as tireless in the making of metaphors will hit upon some good ones, and for every dozen potions of grammar-and-ointment, there will be one superbly expressed and convincing comparison: "[L]ike a spring coiled up, / In the bones of Adam, lay Eve." People who are weary with the magisterial weight of their experiences say that they "bear like ancient marble well-heads / marks of the ropes they lowered us in." In the same poem appears another perfectly visualized analogy that despite its homely reference is touched with magic: A man and woman lie "In a blue vineyard by the Latin sea, / Steeped in each other's minds and breathing there/ Like wicks inhaling deep in golden oil." And here is an example of pure landscape description lightly touched by personification and nicely serrated in its diction: "The islands rebuffed by water. / Estuaries of putty and gold. / A smokeless arc of Latin sky."

These last two excerpts, local yet resonant (the wood fires of old sacrifice notable by their absence), lead to two last points about the quality of Durrell's verse. First, although Durrell is accomplished in the evocation of place and moment, he also wants to philosophize and mythify place—put Dionysus and Pan and time and fate and women-like-Roman-swords into the olive, the estuary, and the island. Like D. H. Lawrence in Mexico, Durrell in the Mediterranean set out to reprimitivize that part of the world so fertile in earlier time, so seemingly refractory to the present. But his very genius for description thwarts his desire to magnify the esoteric meaning of the places he describes.

The second point relates to the first. By inserting precoded programs for feeling into his poems, Durrell evades not only his real gift at description, but also the logic of the poem's development, so that it is much easier to excerpt good parts from his work than it is to point to any one poem and say: This is a complete utterance with its own momentum. Not even his best poems (for example, the Horace poem, "Cities, Plains and People," the superb "Tree of Idleness," "In the Garden: Villa Cleobolus," "Moonlight," and "Deus Loci") make entire sense. Durrell has remained in many ways a half-licked bear, obstinately naive in his double allegiance to exaggeration and to precision. But he has produced a handful of stunning, quirky poems, which I should someday like to see in an anthology like the Norton *Modern Poetry* in place of, say, James Stephens, Austin Clarke, and Samuel Beckett.

Laura Riding *is* represented in the Norton because the poems she wrote in the 1920s were admired by the Fugitives, and because her collaboration with Robert Graves on *A Survey of Modernist Poetry* (1927) initiated or encouraged innovations in literary interpretation. Empson, Ransom, and Brooks were all indebted to the Riding/Graves critique; and although her poetry has not found many imitators, at least one poet sympathetic to some of Riding's early techniques of flattening texture with abstractions, joining hard consonant sounds together, effortlessly coining neologisms, and using plain words in delicately twisted syntax, has had an almost incalculable influence on modern poetry. Now whether W. H. Auden stole from Laura Riding or not, it is clear that what in Riding remained an inward and self-revolving technique becomes in Auden a rhetorical method for satirizing the modern temper. Riding was interested in making strange the words for her own story, Auden in judging shared behavior.

With respect to their comrades in art, writers generally fall into two groups, those who praise writers most like themselves (the enclave tendency) and those who are drawn to writers who are least like themselves (the need to protect by fending off attention from an enclave of one). Laura Riding belonged to the second group to the extent that she found threatening the experiments with a small vocabulary, incantation, and narrow wordplay of Gertrude Stein—experiments that resembled her own. Both Stein and Riding were repelled by pretty adjectives, Swinburnian settings, and obvious tropes (especially simile), although this fact does not distinguish them from scores of poets at the turn of the century who were fed up with Victorian embellishment. But there was a particularly rabid American wave of modernism in the 1920s that broke with what Hardy called the jewelled Tennysonian line more radically than did Hardy, Edward Thomas, or even Pound. On this wave were cast up e. e. cummings, Riding, and Gertrude Stein, whom Laura Riding called "a barbarian," a writer who worked toward "mass-originality . . . without her ordinariness being destroyed." But in fact, says Riding, Stein is "completely without originality. . . . She uses language automatically to record pure, ultimate obviousness" (*Contemporaries and Snobs*, 1928).

Riding did not go as far as Stein did in humming her language to death, but she was prone to effects only slightly less narcotic:

> The little quids, the monstrous quids,
> The everywhere, everything, always quids,
> The atoms of the Monoton,
> Each turned an essence where it stood,
> Ground a gisty dust from its neighbours' edges,
> Until a powdery thoughtfall stormed in and out—
> The cerebration of a slippery quid enterprise.
>
> ("The Quids")

> 'Poor John, John, John, John, John,'
> Said the parson as he perched
> On the sharp left discomfort
> Of John John's tombstone—
> John, John, John, John, John.
>
> ("Lying Spying")

> His luck was perhaps no luck.
> I am a fine fellow.

My good luck is perhaps no luck.
All luck is perhaps no luck.
All luck is luck or perhaps no luck.

          ("The Lullaby")

What to say when I
When I or the spider
No I and I what
Does what does dies
Death spider death
Death always I
Death before always

          ("Elegy in a Spider's Web")

These excerpts indicate a problem that persists in better poems. Like Emily Dickinson and (to a degree) Christina Rossetti, Riding is essentially a writer of the small *mot*, the epigram, the poem of a few lines. Yet *The Poems of Laura Riding* is composed of poems that average between twenty and thirty-five lines. Since her thought has a short round, most of her poems have to start over again halfway through, giving them that hint of casuistry, of bombast and self-importance, that are inevitable when somebody continues to hold the floor after they have finished talking. Riding lacked that regard for stylistic integrity that even the most eccentric modernist poets like Marianne Moore and e. e. cummings and Pound applied so skillfully in the breaking of it. To break a mold, to raise the pitch of an argument, something must be there to be broken, or broken from.

This background of continuity is what Riding's poems miss. For example, the first stanza of the following poem does all that an epigrammatic poem should do, namely, it charms, it points, it suggests. The second stanza blunders through that established delicacy and reiterates more harshly the same point that was better made in the first stanza; the only new idea added in the second is that of following at a slower pace. While the third stanza, whatever its charm, is of a rhetoric more antique, self-conscious, and childish ("No harm is meant," "the thighs / Are meek"):

Without dressmakers to connect
The good-will of the body
With the purpose of the head,
We should be two worlds
Instead of a world and its shadow
The flesh.

The head is one world
And the body another—
The same, but somewhat slower
And more dazed and earlier,
The divergence being corrected
In dress.

There is an odour of Christ
In the cloth: below the chin
No harm is meant. Even, immune
From capital test, wisdom flowers
Out of the shaded breast, and the thighs
Are meek.

("Because of Clothes")

This poem has three more stanzas, each neutral to the others
by virtue of similar disjunctions in sense and tone.

Riding and Graves make an interesting observation in
their *Survey of Modernist Poetry* that could be adjusted for the
poetry of Laura Riding. After getting rid of form imposed
from without, modern poets sought "some principle of . . .
government from within." This was (in circular fashion) free
verse. Formal metrical poetry had an external government
that could endlessly lap the miles of any thematic materials,
hence the natural extension of formal poetry to long poems
(the *Aeneid*, *In Memoriam*), which had no need to work at
transitions. A poem like *The Waste Land*, on the other hand,
since it refrained from inducing the anticipation of regularly
recurring verse patterns, had to forge each transition by
hand, moving from theme to theme, mood to mood, on the
back of deeply pondered associations and echoes. Therefore,
Riding and Graves argue, *The Waste Land* is really just a 433-
line short poem.

I think this idea can also work in reverse for the poem that has no transitions. Riding's "Because of Clothes" is really a thirty-six line *Sartor Resartus*, that is, a long work trapped in the wrong short form. Riding uses in poetry material that is never made poetic, and yet the poems are not energetic enough to extend themselves out to their proper length. Her rejection of poetry in 1938, motivated in part by the deterioration of the Graves ménage, may also have been grounded in this fact, that her impulse was not to write poems at all, but the prose discourses and meditations on body, mind, language, and union, which she has indeed written for the past forty years.

Riding has also during this period become her own advocate in quasi-mystical apologias about her place in literature and her meaning for the history of words. The career of this writer has a psychological dimension that is hard to put delicately: She was an arrogant and impatient poet, in many ways juvenile in the estimation of her importance, in her endless poetic divagations about the right kind of pain, the right kind of strangeness, and the right kind of language, and in her repeated challenges to the reader and the lover that they work hard to discover the exact nuance of her meaning: "Come, words, away: / I am a conscience of you / Not to be held unanswered past / The perfect number of betrayal. / It is a smarting passion / By which I call— / Wherein the calling's loathsome as / Memory of man-flesh over-fondled / With words like over-gentle hands."

The smarting passion of Laura Riding no longer makes much difference to the world of letters, and we cannot help but regret the dead wood in this massive and second-rate oeuvre, from which so often the small gems of precision blink: "I moved the soldier-lusts in you: / Thus did you honour me" ("After Smiling"). Consider also "Fresh year of time, desire, / Late year of my age, renunciation— / Ill-mated pair, debating if the window / Is worth leaping out of, and by whom" ("In Nineteen Twenty-Seven"), and "What is to cry out? / It is to make gigantic / Where speaking cannot last long" ("As Many Questions As Answers").

Daryl Hine has a much greater variety of subject and of linguistic manner than most of his contemporaries. He is a classics scholar and translator, and one of the few poets since Auden at home with the shadow play of classical meters in English. His poetry is so skillful in one sense that, at least in the two volumes since *Minutes* (1968), the germ of feeling and judgment can be lost beneath the ripple of the muscles. There is a virtuoso stubborn streak in Hine that will bind him to the completion of a poetic project more engaging, perhaps, in the conception than in the execution. "Vowel Movements," for example, has thirteen hexameter stanzas, twelve of them devoted to each of the twelve vowel sounds (five long, five short, two diphthongs) and rhyming on that one vowel, and it concludes with a stanza serially composed of single lines from each of the twelve foregoing stanzas:

> Amazing graces that always used to end in mate!
> Precious as sex is, flesh, perennially wretched,
> In fact turns out to be a tourist trap at last.
> The mathematical vision which built this system
> Of the universe, all devouring powerhouse,
> (The mysteries of dust are nothing to live up to!)
> Briefly yields to the weaker tyranny of weeds.
> You used to choose the rules with superfluous humour:
> Monotony, the awful drawback of my song,
> Slowly unfolded, like a brocade robe thrown over.
> Persuaded of the possibility of joy,
> Finally I tried to define why divine silence . . .

This last stanza, despite its broken heritage, almost makes sense. The poet's lines are so frequently *mots* in themselves—syntactically contained, based on the adjective and the noun—that they easily lend themselves to this kind of arbitrary transportation. But the poem itself is so conscious of its surface arrangement that the reader, too, is soon more concerned to see whether Hine is obeying the rules than to ask what the game is about.

The game also obscures the goal in "Linear A" (twenty-five crypto-textual poems under the letters of the Greek alphabet), "*Arrondissements*" (of which there are twenty), not to mention the expectation exerted by a proper sestina called "The Destruction of Sodom" with the trochaic nouns *vices, imagina-*

*tion, cities, perversion, bodies, uses.* There is no difficult form Hine has not tried, few demanding narrative or dramatic constraints he is unwilling to place upon himself, and seemingly no end to the stanza forms he can adjust and reinvent. He writes love lyrics and epistles, satires and odes, the high line and the middle line, and can do what too few wits can, be genuinely funny. The only tone to which his music is not fitted is a tone of unpresuming gentleness.

Most characteristically, especially in his more recent work, Hine attempts to make a virtue out of petty aversions, pulls hard enough at the thread of etymology that the words burst apart like confetti bombs, alliterates with exhausting brio, expresses the last sigh from a catchphrase and puns shamelessly ("Phoenix Culpa," "ilk and money," "a throne's stowaway"), and ornaments his topiary gardens with little deities of appetite and pique.

On the other hand, his handling of simplicity is to rarefy it, even if he wishes to make an entire poem obedient to such subtle dictates. One of Hine's loveliest inventions is the child of "Bluebeard's Wife" (Hine is, incidentally, remarkably sympathetic to the female character), yet in both of her settings—the elegant but sinister grounds laid out by the pirate and the rhymed Spenserian stanzas laid out by the poet—her progress is foreordained. Because of the illusion of freedom in a realm that is rigid, this evocation of childhood is especially poignant:

> The open doors of summer afternoons,
> The scented air that passes in and out
> Ferrying insects, humming with the tunes
> That nature sings unheard! She could not doubt
> She was unseen, no one was about . . .
> . . . . . . . . . . . . . . . . . . . . . . . . . . . . .
> Now she attained the room of artifice.
> Not a thing that grew there but was made:
> Venetian glass that counterfeited ice
> So close it seemed to melt, and green brocade,
> The wind's most subtle movements in a glade.
> . . . . . . . . . . . . . . . . . . . . . . . . . . . . . . .
> Dazzled, she shut the door, but through the next

Saw greater good than any she had seen:
A window open on the sacred text
Of natural things, whose number had not been
Created or conceived, nor did they mean
Other than what they were, splendid and strange.
One leaf is like another, and between
Them all the worlds of difference range;
The world is not destroyed and does not cease to change.

("Bluebeard's Wife")

I can only envy those who have yet to read the final stanza
after this one. What I have quoted will, however, convince
even the most casual reader of the marvelous suppleness of
line, deftness of syntax, and fine coordination between
thought and example with which Hine breathes life into the
Perrault fairy tale.

"Vaugirard," the fifteenth *"Arrondissement,"* shows the very
different, later manner of Hine, ruthless in the portrayal of
fault, yet aloof if not aimless in its intentions. The final two
lines, however, save the poem. Logically resolute, they are also
emotionally direct:

### XV Vaugirard

*Tabula Rasa*, fair and vacant page,
Impenetrable open book unlined
By the ineradicable afterthoughts of age,
Inane impressions that outrage
The paper void its blankness can't defend,
What an idea, to be defined
According to what the petty average
And calculated meanness of mankind,
Catalogued, confined
Captive in a cage,
Cosily conventional, of kind,
A jejune personage
Whose very emptiness may yet engage
The spirit when the flesh is out of mind.

Like this jejune personage, perversely cherished despite es-
sential vacuity, the beloved in many of Hine's major poems

requires his eventual relinquishment. This is true of "*Coma Berenices*" as decided a masterpiece of Hine's middle age as "The Wound" was striking among the love poems of his youth. Unlike the earlier work, "*Coma Berenices*" is both slightly baroque in its variation on phrase and proverb, and more colloquial:

> Faint spark, you were a part once of the darkness,
> About to be absorbed into the sun,
> Shining in inimitable witness,
> A landmark of love's perihelion;
> As my passion for you glows and crumbles,
> A fading coal that used to be a flame,
> A nightmare we can neither alter
> Nor, even if we wanted to, relive
> . . . . . . . . . . . . . . . . . . . . . . . . .
> That love of which you were the incarnation,
> Which could not even really spell its name,
> Idle, illiterate, and infantile,
> Still in the sky of my imagination
> Burns with unmitigated flair,
> Like a lock of Berenice's hair.

Such emotional command in verse is as rare as the courage with which the impossibility of the attachment is faced. The waning of hope has a late-Latin feeling much like that in Kavafis, although the still defiant flare of memory is a fool-hardy flourish, a hopeless tribute, that could only have come from Daryl Hine.

The first poem I read by Janet Lewis appeared in 1980 in the *New Republic*, and on a first reading its externally developed analogies struck me as dated. It was only the last pair of lines that drew me back to the body of the poem for another try, since they were so contrary in their wisdom. What I found then was at once obvious and subtle—a pair of visions, one that said love was absolute, disembodied, and concentrated, another that said love was an incomplete, cyclical process of growth. In the one, the rainbow was implicit, and in the other it was embodied. The abstract view is dreamed, the material view found:

Love is a constant
Like the speed of light,
Unbroken spectrum
Of the purest white,
Rainbow unbroken
In the beam of light.

Love is an anguish
That, gathering at the root,
Rises in sap along the rugged branch,
Pulsing in sunlight,
To lose itself in fruit,
To break in fragrance
Above the sunny ground,
Like wine in autumn,
Like insect wings unbound,
Like wings of gauze and rainbow.

Or so I dreamed
Or so I found.

Both definitions use visual imagery to express the temporal; the beams of light represent that aspect of love that is instantaneous, and eternal, while the arduous chemistry of maturation represents that aspect of love fruitful over the long haul if one is patient. One view says we are visited from without, the other that we must struggle from within. In the first comparison, love is an order, a law; in the second it is a blind impulse.

But here the distinctions begin to be less crucial than the resemblances, for both definitions entail the concept of natural law. Light moves in a prescribed way; so does sap. Neither process is better or purer than the other. Both are phenomena and can be found, yet both are dreams—metaphors—for the emotion that both strikes like lightning and takes a lifetime to perfect. The truth lies between finding and dreaming, light and wine.

The thematic relations are tempered by slight modulations in rhythm and tone—the poem does not have a wide rhetorical sweep. The speaker's individuality is only very softly asserted, and in its modesty, its unassuming courtesy to the tradition of love poetry and song, Lewis's "Words for a Song" takes more risks than many a more breathless and eccentric work. It does not attempt a revolution in language; none of the words has been rescued from its ordinary meanings, and yet the mind at work in the poem, having declared the boundaries to its self-expression, is authoritative and serene.

The authority that Janet Lewis obtains from the simple is what gives her poems their pathos. She reminds us that many poets, with all their particulars, stand between us and the light of pure feeling. In her best work this poet lets through, in language so exact and melodious we think we have always known the words, the simple truths of our being. In an Egyptian museum, the amulets and gems laid out in cases are the "talismans of death":

> All that the anguished mind
> Most nobly could invent,
> To one devotion bent,
> That death seem less unkind;
> That the degraded flesh,
> Grown spiritless and cold,
> Be housed in beaten gold,
> A rich and rigid mesh.
>
> Such pain is garnered here
> In every close-locked case,
> Concentrate in this place
> Year after fading year,
> That, while I wait, a cry,
> As from beneath the glass,
> Pierces me with "Alas
> That the beloved must die!"
>
> ("In the Egyptian Museum")

Here even the archaism is subdued to its context; none of the older usages ("Concèntrate" as a truncated past participle, hence stressed on the second syllable; "a cry / As from"; "Alas / That") is allowed to rise far from the stylistic mean, which in this poem is middle style, so that the final quatrain with that piercing cry sounds (as it was meant to) spoken rather than written.

Lewis increasingly wrote in the middle style after her marriage to Yvor Winters, and also composed a number of poems in the dry, stately Wintersian pentameter line. It is interesting to compare their matching poems, Lewis's "The Hangar at Sunnyvale: 1937" with Winters's "An Elegy for the U.S.N. Dirigible, *Macon*"; Lewis's "Carmel Highlands" with Winters's "The Slow Pacific Swell"; Lewis's "For John Muir" with Winters's "On Rereading a Passage from John Muir." In all these cases, Winters writes the heavier line, with the heavier and broader theme, Lewis the more contented vision. But these are not her best poems, while the first two mentioned happen to be two of Winters's best works.

Although Janet Lewis is deft at the original comparison— "I felt myself like the flame / Of a candle fanned / By every passionate claim, / Flickering fast, / Or brought to an upright stand / In the curve of a hand,"—I think I prefer her least embellished free-verse poems, especially the early poems about the Ojibwa Indians—poems of intimate, haiku-like restraint: "The deer went over the grass / With wet hooves / To the water to drink. // Their shadows passed / Our tent" ("The Grandmother Remembers"). And a final example of Lewis's control and precision, in a small poem that shows you what you are looking at while something remarkable has occurred in the mind of the one who was not looking:

### The Reader

Sun creeps under the eaves,
And shines on the bare floor
While he forgets the earth.

Cool ashes on the hearth,
And all so still save for
The soft turning of leaves.

A creature fresh from birth
Clings to the screen door,
Heaving damp heavy wings.

It is doubtful whether, in a culture like ours where the epic forms and the comprehensive themes have been so thoroughly evolved, any poet of such small effects could be called "great." Perhaps in the Orient Janet Lewis would have grown into her diadem.

## NOTES

1. Donald Hall has brought to my attention the considerable reputation Prince enjoys owing to Oscar Williams's inclusion of "Soldiers Bathing" in his anthologies. Indeed, it would seem to have established Prince as a one-poem poet. "Soldiers Bathing" first appeared in *New Poems 1944: An Anthology of American and British Verse, with a Selection of Poems from the Armed Forces*, ed. Oscar Williams (New York: Howell, Soskin, 1944), where Prince is identified as "British, Captain, Intelligence Corps, M.E.F." Thereafter, it appeared in Williams's editions *A Little Treasury of Modern Poetry, English and American* (New York: Charles Scribner's Sons, 1946), *A Little Treasure of British Poetry: The Chief Poets from 1500 to 1950* (New York: Charles Scribner's Sons, 1951), and in the multiple editions of *A Pocket Book of Modern Verse* (New York: Washington Square Press, 1954 ff.). The poem is discussed below.

2. W. F. Jackson Knight, trans., *The Aeneid* (Harmondsworth: Penguin, 1958), 6:70ff.

# The Forgotten Modernist

Essays were written about her by every major poet of her time except Yeats. She materially inspired the work of Elizabeth Bishop, Louise Bogan (to a degree), and I see a profound kinship between her and John Ashbery. She edited the *Dial* in the 1920s, and in her later years was published by both the *New Yorker* and *Life*. George Plimpton has written about escorting her to the World Series in 1964, and in the 1950s the Ford Motor Company solicited her advice in naming a new car. (Her suggestions, including "chaparral," "mongoose civique," and "pastelogram," were rejected in favor of Ford's misbegotten "Edsel.") Yet despite both later public renown and (what I take to be earlier) poetic achievement, Marianne Moore (1887–1972) is seldom assigned and rarely mentioned at the university where I teach, I think because she is an original whose erudition is idiosyncratic in a way most readers no longer understand or admire.

Marianne Moore's greatest idiosyncrasy is to have combined in her art two literary extremes, energetically forging together pithy brevity with prosaic expansiveness. She is frequently compared to Emily Dickinson, few of whose poems exceed 20 lines (Moore's longest is nearly 300), and whose subject (yearning for transcendence) is powerfully opposed, or echoed in reverse, by her diminutive stanzas. Like Dickinson, Marianne Moore was taken with the minutiae of a contemplative and restricted existence; in fact, both tended, in their mediocre work, toward the fussy tones of the "maiden

Review of Marianne Moore, *The Complete Poems of Marianne Moore* (New York: Macmillan/Viking, 1981).

lady." Both teach us, however, that the ordinary becomes the exotic only by way of enormous pressure of wit, striving for combustion. Each was a loyal reader of devotional literature, so that even domestic details were expressive of the secret workings of the divine. And although both poets showed great insight into human psychology, neither narrated others' lives. At most, the habits of others were made to glance off the prism of metaphor, with effects of great rapidity and hard justice.

But Marianne Moore does things in her poems that cannot be educed from her affinity with Dickinson, who is usually singing. Moore, like her other avatar, Henry James, principally talks. Like James, she dwells lovingly on any evidence of character—although, instead of an exclusive focus on the man-made, Moore attends to any plant, animal, or rock formation that seems to her expressive of our national turn of mind. Interpolating remarks from a U. S. Department of the Interior pamphlet and John Ruskin, she describes the chilly landscape around Mt. Rainier: "The fir-trees, in 'the magnitude of their root systems,' / rise aloof . . . 'creepy to behold,' / austere specimens of our American royal families, / 'each like the shadow of the one beside it.' " In a seaside New England town, where the Gulf Stream produces "the tropics at first hand," the stalwart wit of the villagers is represented by a small indigenous lizard: "The diffident / little newt / with white pin-dots on black horizontal spaced- / out bands lives here; yet there is nothing that / ambition can buy or take away." Her emphasis is anti-exotic in theme, but not in form.

In her poems about animals, Marianne Moore is not writing psychological fables like La Fontaine, for her "fables" are not fixed on plot. She is making emblems for habits of imaginative possession. In good light and bad, the natural world exhibits the intellectual, familial, and conversational gestures of decorum, which is the balance of cultivation with goodness. And, in a real sense, human beings are the covering presences for the animal poems, growing or diminishing by implied association. These are usually the three points of reference in a Moore poem, the animal, or natural; the human; and the moral-formal. The line that joins the three points could be viewed as an unequal triangle whose second point is reached by first touching the third. "To a Snail" is the clearest rendering of the triangular star made by the natural world as the human realm absorbs it under the sign of inspired sympathy. Whereas the following brief poem is the most brilliant and musical rendering of the three movable centers:

*An Egyptian Pulled Glass Bottle in the Shape of a Fish*

Here we have thirst
and patience, from the first,
    and art, as in a wave held up for us to see
    in its essential perpendicularity;

not brittle but
intense—the spectrum, that
    spectacular and nimble animal the fish,
    whose scales turn aside the sun's sword by their polish.

As for the value of this particular new volume: It is simply the only game in town. I thought the paperback *Marianne Moore Reader* (1965) was flawed by leaning too heavily toward the later poetry, although the selections from La Fontaine were wiser and more generous, and the essays and correspondence were marvelous. But that, too, is out of print. This edition contains only five poems not printed in a subsequent edition that was also called *Complete* (1967) and is now also out of print; these are slight, though three have nice turns ("Mercifully," "Enough," and "The Magician's Retreat"). But in order to make room for these, the La Fontaine has been pared down from nine to five fables that will hardly endear the new reader to this massive and embattled translation. There are changes in the notes between 1967 and 1981, but quite minor ones. The text itself undergoes changes in lineation, as in the superb "Those Various Scalpels," which must now have more different rhythmic incarnations than any of Moore's poems. In general, however, the textual changes involve hyphenation.

Above all, this edition is timidly conservative. Still missing is the poem T. S. Eliot printed in *Selected Poems* in 1935 and the one most often cited by critics, "Black Earth" (aka "Melancthon"), along with the lucid companion to "Marriage" called

"Roses Only." Three admittedly lesser short poems, the hardly minor three middle stanzas of "The Frigate Pelican," in which a magically guarded landscape unfolds beneath the bird, and the earlier versions of poems like "Those Various Scalpels" and "Peter," which lineated by rhyme, are still absent in this "complete" edition. However, the first 140 pages of the 1981 volume, through "Nevertheless" (1944), continue to offer the best available introduction to the best work of an eccentric genius in whom prose complication was a servant to poetic truth.

# Native Voices

Among poets who write in form, there are some who can take hold of one or two rhymes and, with these necessarily makeshift tools, hammer out the themes of their own particular fates. In fact, we can identify some poets if given only the pairs of rhyme words around which a characteristic poem turns. Thus we can recognize the twilight melancholy of Tennyson in the rhyme of *tears* with *years*. At the sound of the off-rhyme, itself tortuous, between *true* and *throe*, the figure of Emily Dickinson steps forth. A. E. Housman's twin disappointments, in his career and in his loves, logically connect the random consonance between *mad* and *lad*. Even if you haven't read Yeats since school, you may easily associate him with such pairs as *beautiful/fool*, *horn/born*, and *quarrel/laurel*.

Robert Lowell's tendency to toss rhymes off yields the smoothly conservative syntax of the rhymes between like parts of speech, *aground/drowned*, *cell/hell*, *God/Cape Cod*, and *skull/hull*; the wit and energy come from his dramatization of the implied themes, as well as from a new specificity of vocabulary. W. H. Auden is playing a different if not subtler game, because he brings to bear on any rhyme the whole of the phrase of which the rhyme-word is a part, as in the brilliant conjunction between those words of human contract in "The Shield of Achilles," *kept* and *wept*—the first reminding us of Frost stopping alone by his neighbor's woods, and the second suggesting a warmer and more intimate redemption:

---

Review of Derek Walcott, *The Fortunate Traveler* (New York: Farrar, Straus & Giroux, 1981).

That girls are raped, that two boys knife a third,
Were axioms to him, who'd never heard
Of any world where promises were kept,
Or one could weep because another wept.

Like these poets, the West Indian Derek Walcott may have given us his own capsule aesthetics in the rhyme between *beach* and *speech*. Like Lowell's, this rhyme is syntactically bland, since each word is a noun; but it differs from Lowell's in that it raises the issue of passive materiality (*beach*) versus active interpretation (*speech*). Hence the play between thing and act is invoked without flexing the sentence structure, producing a curiously paralyzed fluency in such descriptions as,

> Your forehead was as unmarked beach
> . . . . . . . . . . . . . . . . . . . . . . . . . . . . .
> In your speech
> Was the clearness of the curled wave,
> Green crystal in dead of noon,
> In it was neither cunning nor subtlety.
>
> ("Pays Natal," 1962)

The clarity of the woman's Antilles patois is a negative value, lacking goal or shade, as if the land with which she is associated were also, in its very substance, vacant. The meagerness is both linguistic and historical. As Walcott writes in his long autobiographical poem *Another Life* (1973), historian and anthropologist find but slim pickings amid the islands' epic, mindless decay: "[T]he lizards are taking a million years to change, / and the lopped head of the coconut rolls to gasp on the sand, / its mouth open at the very moment / of forgetting its name."

Even as Walcott is consoled by the King's English for the loss of the lilting patois of his childhood, he wants to turn this standard tongue upon the very reality that, as it tries to speak, forgets its own name. For three decades, however, from 1948 to 1979, Walcott wrote correct and derivative colonial verse, reserving dialect, patois, and jive for his plays. The first time he makes a sustained effort to combine the two sides of his personality is in the remarkable dramatic monologue that opens his 1979 volume, *The Star-Apple Kingdom*. Spoken by a mulatto sailor from Trinidad named Shabine, "The Schooner *Flight*" is an electrifying adjustment of the decasyllable line to the special frequency of Walcott's native voice:

> You ever look up from some lonely beach
> and see a far schooner? Well, when I write
> this poem, each phrase go be soaked in salt;
> I go draw and knot every line as tight
> as ropes in this rigging; in simple speech
> my common language go be the wind,
> my pages the sails of the schooner *Flight*.

In his new volume, *The Fortunate Traveller*, Walcott takes the lyrical voice of Shabine and gives him an even more dramatic presence as the carnival Creole nicknamed "Spoiler," whom Satan sends back to Laventville as a scout. Spoiler describes himself as "Bedbug the First," "the flea whose itch to make all Power wince, / will crash a fête, even at his life's expense." This *honnête homme* with a touch of the satiric devil in him—a composite persona also used by Rochester, Dryden, and Byron—has a personal stake in the geopolitics of the Caribbean:

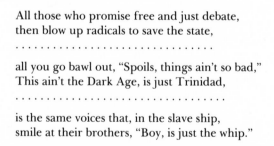

> All those who promise free and just debate,
> then blow up radicals to save the state,
> ·····························
> all you go bawl out, "Spoils, things ain't so bad,"
> This ain't the Dark Age, is just Trinidad,
> ································
> is the same voices that, in the slave ship,
> smile at their brothers, "Boy, is just the whip."

At the other extreme from the calypso couplets of the Spoiler, Walcott speaks in his own voice in "North and South" and "The Hotel Normandie Pool"—poems about the bitter roots and remnants of his inheritance. Just as the rhyme of *speech* with *beach* shadows his relation to themes as much as to forms, so Walcott's allusiveness always points beyond merely literary debts to touch those forefathers whom he describes in an early poem as having "drunkenly seeded the archipelago." His own "randy white grandsire" still chars his skin with shame: "My skin sears like a hairshirt with his name." Now in "North and South," on a trip through the States, racial crimes are treated yet more literally as flames. Even in wintry Virginia he smells something burning: Treblinka, a Klansman's cross, dark holocausts. These associations recombine with at least a dozen more in the final stanza, among them Ovid's exile on the Black Sea, the Diaspora, the burning of Carthage, coming down with the flu, the demise of the Roman Empire and the British Raj, and the statue of Sheridan that reminds Walcott of each island port's statue of Victoria. Walcott also puns on the French for monkey (*un singe*), which is visually identical to the unrelated English *singe* (or *scorch*), to conjure up the stereotype of the black jazz artist, playing for coins:

> But in Virginia's woods there is also an old man
> dressed like a tramp in an old Union greatcoat,
> walking to the music of rustling leaves, and when
> I collect my change from a small-town pharmacy,
> the cashier's fingertips still wince from my hand
> as if it would singe hers—well, yes, *je suis un singe*,
> I am one of that tribe of frenetic or melancholy
> primates who made your music for many more moons
> than all the silver quarters in the till.
>
> ("North and South")

To be sure, the full elegiac and satiric flavor of these lines cannot be felt without more extensive reference to the accumulations in the poem's previous thirteen stanzas. Indeed, dependence on cumulative rather than immediate meaning is one of the most peculiar qualities of Walcott's verse, and in his minor poems creates an effect of unnecessary depths, as if great blocks of meaning were amalgamating somewhere way beneath the threshold of our notice.

But the doubling occurs strongly in Walcott's larger undertakings, and not only in the weave of single poems: It can also span suites, sections and entire books. The leaf-littered cobbles of Europe wink in the rain from several poems here; so do the flames of suffering, which reach their lurid height in the Jacobean darkness of the title poem. And in the most striking example of the leitmotif that becomes a "rhyme" joining disparate poems, the song of birds stitches or weaves a world as an emblem of pain; Ovid in exile is the first to notice how yearning pricks the soul:

> "Through shaggy pines the beaks of needling birds
> pricked me at Tomis to learn their tribal tongue,
> so, since desire is stronger than its disease,
> my pen's beak parted till we chirped one song."

From Ovid's voice in stanza sixteen, Walcott in the last of the poem's twenty-one stanzas shifts to his own voice speaking the exile's withdrawing coda. The moment is full of fear at the silvery refractions and the throbbing dusk in which "something, not a leaf, falls like a leaf, / as swifts with needle-beaks dart, panicking over / the pool's cloud-closing light," and "The fruit bat swings on its branch, a tongueless bell."

The sick fright of this modern poet invoking his exiled Roman mentor beside a pool has found expression in metaphors of flickering existences. This sense of hovering animal life is magnified numerically in "The Fortunate Traveler," where the race of diplomats is said by the sinister narrator to resemble swarms of roaches infesting "cabinets"; similarly, the world's starving millions compose swarms of flies "who shed glazed wings" and "seethe" about a tree. The massing of these human swarms is an echo—or an off-rhyme—of the earlier darting panic of the birds at dusk. After these ghostly swarms have faded, the final poem in Walcott's new book opens:

> Then all the nations of birds lifted together
> the huge net of the shadows of this earth
> in multitudinous dialects, twittering tongues,
> stitching and crossing it. . . .
>
> ("The Season of Phantasmal Peace")

As if the valence of the title poem had been changed, by a powerful magnet, from damnation to grace, the swarms and

plagues have been transformed into flocks of birds again, who
stitch the world together for a phantasmal season:

> and this season lasted one moment, like the pause
> between dusk and darkness, between fury and peace,
> but, for such as our earth is now, it lasted long.

Beautiful as these lines are, their pathos is harmoniously aug-
mented by the other flocks of echoes from which, in his best
poems, Derek Walcott stitches his matter into song.

# From "Haunting"

With *The Southern Cross*, Charles Wright moves into a rich tropic crosshatched with patterns at once civilized (the gem-bright labyrinths of Venice) and naturally lush (quasi-savage blossoming vegetation of the sort that flourishes in latitudes where the Southern Cross is prominent in the night sky). Wright romanticizes immediate locale in all the journeys, traced in so many poems, from rest to intense engagement with ethereal thresholds, tints of light, floating gestures—"an incandescent space," he says in one poem, "where nothing distinct exists, / And nothing ends, the days sliding like warm milk through the clouds." I quote these lines because they make explicit the poet's preference for the hazy, the milky, the upper-atmospheric; these are the trappings of his transcendent states of infancy.

I use the term "infancy" advisedly. Charles Wright's apotheoses are characteristically visions of a pre-sexual, light-suffused mist, the matrix of dreams and the medium of serenity and soaring, of effortless floating, a rising upwards that is very much more pleasant but far less emotionally pressing than either the multiplicitous harmonies of Derek Walcott or the sultry risings and impassioned upwellings and poolings in the poems of contemporaries like Louise Glück. Whereas Walcott is fused to history while Glück returns to the profound tensions and jealousies of childhood, Wright explores an al-

---

Review of Charles Wright, *The Southern Cross* (New York: Random House, 1981); Mona Van Duyn, *Letters from a Father, and Other Poems* (New York: Atheneum, 1982); Katha Pollitt, *Antarctic Traveller* (New York: Alfred A. Knopf, 1982).

most fetal suspended state just prior to birth. The superbly ambitious title poem of *The Southern Cross* ends in Pickwick, Tennessee, at the moment the narrator is born:

> Somewhere in all that network of rivers and roads and silt hills,
> A city I'll never remember,
> > its walls the color of pure light,
> Lies in the August heat of 1935,
> In Tennessee, the bottom land slowly becoming a lake.
> It lies in a landscape that keeps my imprint
> Forever,
> > and stays unchanged, and waits to be filled back in.
> Someday I'll find it out
> And enter my old outline as though for the 1st time,
>
> And lie down, and tell no one.

The desire to return to the softer outline he had at the beginning before experience marked him with choice and error and the plain banality of repetition emerges over and over again in Wright's new volume. As he travels backward in time toward his origins, he is also preparing for his death, expressed as a reduction to infant dependency. Here, in 1938, he has moved as far as Knoxville:

> I hope the one with the white wings will come.
> I hope the island of reeds is as far away as I think it is.
>
> When I get there, I hope they forgive me if the knot I tie is
> > the wrong knot.
> > > ("Hawaii Dantesca")

One of the voices Wright invokes is Dante's, from those two books of the *Comedy* whose imagery and exempla are paler and less violent than the *Inferno*'s. As epigram to *The Southern Cross*, Wright quotes Statius's homage to Vergil from the twenty-first canto of *Purgatory*; Statius ruefully admits that his love of the Master had enflamed him to treat a shade as a solid thing. In the excerpt from "Hawaii Dantesca" above, Wright's narrator puts off for the little island of reeds of *Purgatory I* where Cato advises Dante to be cleansed. And in the beautiful "Laguna Dantesca," the poet slips off into the great sea of being of the beginning of the *Paradiso*, piloting his little bark after Dante's into the intermittent cloud dazzle that Dante describes as lucid, dense, solid, and polished (*Par. II*) and in which he sees pale, pearly faces he thinks are mirrored from behind him, so faint are they (*Par. III*). One of these faces belongs to Piccarda Donati, a nun of the Clares, who, having told her story begins (while singing "Ave Maria") to vanish like something heavy falling through deep water. Here is Charles Wright's working of some of these images:

> I want, like a little boat, to be isolate,
>
>                              slipping across one element
> Toward the horizon
> . . . . . . . . . . . . . . . .
>
> Like a rock, or some other heavy thing, I want to descend through
>    clear water
> Endlessly,
>            disappearing as she did,
> Line after leached line, into the lunar deeps.
>
>                                 ("Laguna Dantesca")

Although Piccarda was not atoning (being already elevated among the blessed even at a low level), Wright's lyrical "I" returns reflexively to the idea of cleansing as he views his projected sinking through "Line after *leached* line," as if the medium allowed him to filter out the taint of—not wrongdoing or weakness; the realm of this writer is utterly untouched by judgment—but consciousness itself.

Wright reads Dante with the same selective lens he uses for Eugenio Montale and for the third great mentor of the current poems, William Blake; that is, he is intrigued by the tissues of their imagery at its softest, and by their treatment of nostalgia, but not by their anagogy. It is a very selective reading of both Dante and Blake that would ignore both allegories and discourses; and without the earnest attention of an elegist like Montale to other human beings, nostalgia becomes sentimental. In Charles Wright, however, the anagoge is always self—one who happens to be a sensitive lover of beauty, to be sure; and a maker of elegant artifacts, without question; but occasionally an artist, possibly among false spirits (this I can't judge), with decidedly false professions and poses.

The long failed sequence "Homage to Paul Cézanne" so abounds in misjudgments in tone and in tact that the reader is apt to forget that the painter Cézanne is supposed to be central, although there is little in his paintings that the mediumistic dramatizations of these eight poems have touched. Wright posits a community of dead; unlike Dante's or Montale's dead, these dead are specific neither to history nor to the poet's own life; they are a vague body, with no will or direction, that can be made to function like rain, like color, like darkness, like moods, like clothing, like sounds, like premonition. Hence "the dead" are the collective noun for lugubrious poetic feeling. Some of the personifications are quite funny: "Spring picks the locks of the wind"; "spaces / In black shoes, their hands clasped"; "The dead are constant in / The white lips of the sea." Some of the stage props the dead must carry around are also awkwardly amusing: "We filigree and we baste. / But what do the dead care for the fringe of words, / Safe in their suits of milk?" Sometimes it may be simply a garbled phrasing that mars the mythmaking: "under their fingers an unreturnable dirt"; in another poem, "the bears / Amble across the heavens, serene as black coffee."

But there is the more general problem of framework and intention raised by "Homage" and applicable to other poems as well: The poet fails to make his choices of subject, diction, and tone seem always just; at times they do not even sound deliberate. On occasion I have considered that Wright as a craftsman with words, tropes, and sentences is without a built-in censor. He inflates his poetics into mere shapeless benevolence. Nothing is judged, nothing rejected, nothing refused admittance to the poem.

What William Blake offered in 1789 as a negative representation of timidity, Charles Wright exports, two centuries later, as a positive and strong representation of life, I think because for him behavior does not count, nor is religion a living possibility. Here are some representative lines from *The Book of Thel*:

"Ah! Thel is like a wat'ry bow, and like a parting cloud;
"Like a reflection in glass; like shadows in the water;
"Like dreams of infants, like a smile upon an infant's face;
"Like the dove's voice; like transient day; like music in the air.
· · · · · · · · · · · · · · · · · · · · · · · · · · · · · · · · · · · · · · · · · · · · · · · · · · ·
"Thel is like a faint cloud kindled at the rising sun:
"I vanish from my pearly throne, and who shall find my
place?"

Whatever his intentions may have been, Wright recuperates images of passivity much like Blake's, devoting himself to the composition of ephemeral structures about ephemeral tints and passing, filmy, essentially solitary manifestations:

The clouds over the Bardolino dragging the sky for the dead
Bodies of those who refuse to rise,
Their orange robes and flaming bodices trolling across the
hills
· · · · · · · · · · · · · · · · · · · · · · · · · · · · · · · · · · · · · · · · · · · · · · · ·
No sound but the wind from anything
under the tired, Italian stars . . .

And the voice of the waters, starting its ghostly litany.
· · · · · · · · · · · · · · · · · · · · · · · · · · · · · · · · · · · · · · · · · · ·
River of bloom-bursts from the moon,
of slivers and broken blades from
the moon
In an always-going-away of glints . . .
("The Southern Cross")

The complex alliterations and the mimetic river music in the last three lines above are masterful, and the flow, throughout the passage, of a great sensual appetite projecting bodily presence—this, too, is a powerful and lovely effect. But the idea of trolling bodices is at once obscure and inaccurate. Perhaps to read Charles Wright is to accommodate oneself uncomplainingly to these flaws, alongside which, in "Virginia Reel" and in "The Southern Cross" (especially the passages about Venice in all seasons), we frequently have descriptive poetry of great visual power and verbal loveliness.

Mona Van Duyn is a poet both forcefully grim in confronting reality and formally grotesque. There is a quality about her most ambitious work that is perversely unpoetical, as if she were determined to suffer all over again the eclipse of stress by syllable-stress meter, and the emergence of blank verse from the overhanging eaves of rhyme. Thus she will posit an alternating rhyme scheme for pentameter quatrains and then do her best to make what results sound like untutored (not to mention unmetered) prose. The title poem of *Letters from a Father* shows the poet's parents during their last year (both died in 1980), the mother senile and incontinent, the father ailing and irascible. What brings father and daughter together in their letters now is bird watching, or rather, bird feeding, to which the father is won over only with strenuous effort on both their parts; at first, he resists:

> You say you enjoy your feeder, I don't see why
> you want to spend good money on grain for birds
> and you say you have a hundred sparrows, I'd buy
> poison and get rid of their diseases and turds.

These packed and battered quatrains are designed to render a gruff rustic's bedrock earnestness, but I do not find the method compelling as poetry. Van Duyn has given us indeed pitiable portraits of her parents, and of her irreducibly unromantic childhood (though it may be that she simply remembers the cruel and ambiguous dullness of childhood with a clearer head than the rest of us do). But owing to autobiographical confidences no reader can help noticing and being moved by, the poet *corners* us with the same threatening intensity that marked the ancient mariner. It would be inhumane to dismiss the suffering or the persons; but the title poem is not excused by the mimetic fallacy, merely organized by it.

The blank-verse "Photographs" is less rough, whether because rhyme is no longer under attack, or because the poet-narrator is present in the scene, negotiating the descriptive and historical transitions that give a sense of continuing conscious life and sympathy when the father loses interest in one or another snapshot (the mother is in a separate sphere throughout). An interesting feature of the poem is what it reveals (or begins to) about the real demon in the daughter's youth:

> Expressive
> face I studied all my childhood to learn
> if I was wrong or right, kept or cast out.
> Best cook in town, best seamstress—not enough.
> . . . . . . . . . . . . . . . . . . . . . . . . . . . . . . . . . . . .
> the lovely features never show
> her "nerves," the long years of dissatisfaction,
> the walks she took me on when I reached adolescence
> and poured my hard ear full of my father's failings.
>
> ("Photographs")

Van Duyn has also written an elegy for her mother, called "The Stream," which is one of her finest works. Composed in forty-five rapid running couplets, it recounts her last visit with her mother in the nursing home the week before her death. The poet doesn't balk at references to "peeing" and "dugs"; in fact she works the least decorous details into the main Freudian symbol patterns of the poem, the mother as the daughter's child, her mature features having shriveled back against the body, reminding of the diuretic flood of tears that, in the poem's main metaphor (dowsing for water) is produced by grace from underground. The mother apparently expressed love only seldom, but does so directly now, at the end of her life, in one of those lucid intervals peculiar to those who are failing fast. "What is love?" the poet asks; "Truly I do not know . . . Sometimes, perhaps, instead of a great sea, / it is a narrow stream running urgently // far below ground, held down by rocky layers, / the deeds of father and mother, helpless sooth-sayers // of how our life is to be, weighted by clay, / the dense pressure of thwarted needs, the replay // of old misreadings" ("The Stream"). Above these hardened layers of possibility and mistake runs "another seeker" in scatterbrained, will-less fash-ion, moved by a dowsing rod,

which bends, then lifts, dips, then straightens, everywhere,
saying to the dowser, it is there, it is not there,

and the untaught dowser believes, does not believe,
and finally simply stands on the ground above,

till a sliver of stream finds a crack and makes its way,
slowly, too slowly, through rock and earth and clay.

Here at my feet I see, after sixty years,
the welling water—to which I add these tears.

The upwelling of water betokens expression and release; what was so long thwarted and misread is now sped and numinously transparent. And yet the language never becomes intrusively literary; the guise of naturalness is maintained and, especially here at the end, aggrandized. At the same time as the diction is "natural," the rhythms have rounded more flexibly and formally, like wild-looking vines, about the symmetrical oak of the heroic pentameters. Technically speaking, Van Duyn is using the favorite trick of Robert Frost, the folksy sound produced by two slacks in a row (trochaic and anapestic substitution both provide this in an iambic poem), which, instead of sounding rough, quick, *or* anapestic, becomes with clever handling the regular counterpoint rhythm to the abstract binary iambs. The resulting melody is well-suited to a speaker at once unpretentious in style and overbearing in feeling.

Although "The Stream" earns my admiration, there is still about it something slightly forced, which does not arise in idler, less driven poems. For example, "Moose in the Morning, Northern Maine" provides the old tenacity of subject (few poets are more dissatisfied with imagism, the languid aperçu, few better disciplined at tracking an implication down); Van Duyn's typically wacky and off-kilter viewpoint is also in evidence, and, stemming from this, her skill at amalgamating poems out of widely disparate languages but in such a way that, although there is always some oscillation between low and high ("A ton of monarch, / munching, he stands"), the oscillation doesn't sound like a coat of old mythologies. The moose poem invokes old friends, fellow artists, the comedies of rustic discomfort, and the nervous avoidance the poet feels compelled to enact against her own hard-earned and pent-up need to make, while she can, anything and everything into poetry. After flagrantly tagging each danger zone and weak bridge, Van Duyn permits the moose to swim forward:

> The world is warming and lightening
> and mist on the pond
> dissolves into bundles and ribbons.
> At the end of my dock there comes clear,
> bared by the gentle burning,
> a monstrous hulk with thorny head,
> up to his chest in the water,
> mist wreathing round him.
> Grander and grander grows the sun
> until he gleams, his brown coat
> glistens, the great rack,
> five feet wide, throws sparks
> of light. A ton of monarch,
> munching, he stands spotlit.
> Then slowly, gravely, the great neck lowers
> head and forty pounds of horn
> to sip the lake.

That is simply riveting free verse, not only wise and fierce, but faintly amused, as Van Duyn's best poems tend to be. It is only as an aftereffect that we realize how well this quaintly valedictory descriptive poem has celebrated the creaturely harmony Robert Frost chafed against when he was presented with the apparition of the buck in "The Most of It."

The first poem in Katha Pollitt's *Antarctic Traveller*, called "Blue Window," is characterized by smooth junctures and easy speech melodies (qualities that help make the beautiful poem also pronounceable); by an effusion of feeling restrained by realism; and by a consciousness disciplined so as to receive the overtures of the imagination with a calm demeanor. Furthermore, like many of the poems in the book, this is an urban poem, by which I mean neither worldly nor civic. Instead, Pollitt lightly records the complicated rhythms of a sensibility invigorated by large buildings, architectural vistas, endlessly repeating grids, accidentally pleasing arrangements of lights that have been planted for utility rather than to give a far-off viewer pleasure. And she is, finally, attuned to the last seduction of a great city like New York—the suggestion of social complexity and cultivation that can rise, on occasion, to the level of social harmony. In one poem the city becomes the metaphor for looking toward the future ("So many wide plazas, so many marble addresses!"); in another, examples of urban elegance (little palaces; a procession of French schoolgirls like irises) become the collective metaphor for bright, high, clear weather ("I say, Amaze me, amaze me: / these boulevards are streaming. / I move through the light like light").

These urban responses form the implied, half-drawn-in background for many of this poet's most credible movements, like the self-projecting passion of "Blue Window," which begins:

> That longing you have to be invisible,
> transparent as glass, thin air—
> that is what moves you certain times to tears
> watching the evening fill with city lights
> and the long dusty summer avenues
> rise weightless through the air
> and tremble like constellations in a sky
> so deep and clear you are your one desire,
> *Oh, let me be that blue . . .*

In addition to physical-spatial projection into evanescent distance, "Blue Window" also works to render the qualities of bright and dusky light, color, and even the feeling of temperature, in a painterly way. In this Pollitt is like Wallace Stevens, but without his severe metaphysical angle and spareness of scene. Her eye is true and her feeling for composition nice. She includes here a suite of poems on Japanese painting; the last, on Taiga's painting of two old men reminiscing, is especially well done. And her painterly impulse plucks up its own pleasant nerve in this crisp autumnal:

> The sky a shock, the ginkgoes yellow fever,
> I wear the day out walking. November, and still

light stuns the big bay windows on West End
Avenue, the park brims over with light like a bowl
and on the river
a sailboat quivers like a white leaf in the wind.
("November Fifth, Riverside Drive")

This urban-scape uses formal groupings and accents at once compositionally and in the verse patterns. This stanza is actually the inverted sestet of the sonnet, with the short line and several top-heavy enjambments contrasting, by almost marring, the pentameters, while the final line, more regular, and sharp in verbal and rhythmic edge, traces the *visual* accent mark, the distant sail. Pollitt here turns to account a truth known to many Romantic painters and poets alike, that a small vessel far out on the waves is a plangent image of the human soul. We are again reminded of this fact in her uncanny choice of *The Iceberg*, by the nineteenth-century American luminist Frederick Edwin Church, for the cover.

Katha Pollitt often reminds us that her imagination is supported by a medium that is fluid; this support is double, referring us both to her technical responses to the fluid medium of painting and to the fluid vehicles of metaphors whose tenors are light, color, or brilliance. Metaphorically, of course, streams and pools are also necessarily the medium through which not merely light but thought, consciousness, and memory are borne into the present time. The extent to which the city park "brims over with light like a bowl" is also the extent to which thought is rising to the mind, memories to the recollection, and feeling to the organs of release. Still upholding the two values of her "medium," the poet makes explicit the bond between art and feeling, a deepening of significance in one arena welling up spontaneously as an intensification in the other. Her art doesn't feel entirely formed, so may lead to stronger explorations of nuanced particularity.

# Rites of Understatement

Wendell Berry's work is all of a piece—it is also a poetry of monotones. Hence it is the constancy of certain gestures throughout a suite or section that interests, rather than the given poem. The simplicity of style is such as to make us both relish and regret the writer's refusal to try for effects; the style is so imbedded in and interwoven with intelligence that we feel it would effortlessly achieve any sort of local brilliance it could deflect its attention from major concerns *to* achieve. But the style also shuns the frivolity of tendril and sucker; all its energy is held back for the great tree's root and the trunk's girth, bound into the broad columns of living matter.

All the poems are glosses on the one theme: "A man of faithful thought may feel / in light, among the beasts and fields, / the turning of the wheel." The wheel represents symmetry, cyclicality, and justice, to which Berry responds with an almost naive pleasure and none of the fear and nausea that motivate the Buddhist striving for release: "The wheel of eternity is turning / in time, its rhymes, austere, / at long intervals returning, / sing in the mind, not in the ear." Thus although Berry's work is songlike, gentle in its effects, and moderately euphonious, the poet also justifies and promotes its blandness by addressing the mind, and not the ear.

This volume is at once marred and ennobled by its naïveté, simplicity, and redundancy in much the same way these traits, coupled with a plodding metrical facility, contribute to the

---

Review of Wendell Berry, *The Wheel* (San Francisco: North Point Press, 1982); Thom Gunn, *The Passages of Joy* (New York: Farrar Straus Giroux, 1982).

winsome but stolid character of Edwin Arlington Robinson's verse. In his elegy for a farmer with the Robinsonian name of Owen Flood, Wendell Berry permits the ghost of Owen to call up a series of tableaus representing the latter's relationship to the young speaker. In one, "the man and the boy lay / on their backs in the deep grass, quietly / talking. In the distance moved / the outcry of one deep-voiced hound." The trope of feeling is refracted against and through the baying of the hound. In another tableau, "I saw him furious and narrow," but also "saw the virtue / that made him unlike most . . . his passion to be true / to the condition of the Fall— / to live by the sweat of his face, to eat / his bread, assured that the cost was paid." Here I think we come very close to a side of the national character easy to flatten into fanatical stereotype— every election seems to do so—yet treated by the poet with nerve and tact. And in a third tableau (the crown of the sequence) the poet manages Owen's dialogue and the view down the furrow so that each means twice—once literally, then eternally:

> Again, in the sun
> of his last harvest, I heard him say:
> "Do you want to take this row,
> And let me get out of your way?"
> I saw the world ahead of him then
> for the first time, and I saw it
> as he already had seen it,
> himself gone from it.

The lines poignantly render the teaching of the young man by the old one in a parable rich with both presence and reference, the immediate and the eventual tributaries of meaning.

These two streams issue from many of the songs and tales of *The Wheel*. The poet is adept at portraying experience so loyal to its own terms that it slips through them and begins to mean much more. This is the experience or detail Christine Brooke-Rose has called the "literal symbol," and John Bayley a "natural metonymy"—the object so plump and three-dimensional with its own truth as to press beyond to greater truth of feeling, sympathy, and insight. Writers like Thomas Hardy and William Wordsworth are good sources for the literal symbol; so, for all his flatness, is Wendell Berry. Here he describes walking up from a ravine in the early morning:

> I was walking in a dark valley
> and above me the tops of the hills
> had caught the morning light.
> I heard the light singing as it went out
> among the grassblades and the leaves.
> I waded upward through the shadow
> until my head emerged,
> my shoulders were mantled with the light,
> and my whole body came up
> out of the darkness, and stood
> on the new shore of the day.

Although the terms "mantled" and "shore" point to two kinds of metaphoric gloss provided by the poet, the other terms (of darkness, singing, emergence, wholeness, and light) are not really tropes at all but rather literal terms touched and freighted with spontaneous significance.

The second part of the last poem in the book, "The Rain," is a yet more pure example of the literal symbol because here metaphor contributes least to the unfolding texture of the poem:

> The path I follow
> I can hardly see
> it is so faintly trod
> and over grown.
> At times, looking,
> I fail to find it
> among dark trunks, leaves
> living and dead. And then
> I am alone, the woods
> shapeless around me.
> I look away, my gaze
> at rest among leaves,
> and then I see the path
> again, a dark going on
> through the light.

Light is such a powerful spiritual cipher that it throws a pejorative shadow about the newfound path; the speaker sounds disappointed to find it (although he had been looking for it) because his aim, and, with it, appetite, instinct, work, and discipline, had been suspended ("my gaze / at rest"). At the same time, this moment is cut from the larger pattern and hence is not to be exaggerated: This is no hallowed Spot of Time, rather a meditation that arises from faithful thought. That the poem above is only one section in the poem "The Rain" and the longer poem "The Wheel" may say much about its composition—it was not styled as a tour de force—but these can detract nothing from our relish in its excellence. In fact, these conditions school us in scale and decorum as do some kinds of Oriental architecture and design.

Thom Gunn's decorum derives not from disciplines of inwardness but from those of conversation. He is one of the few poets of our day who writes as if he also talks, listens, and looks about him; who gives the impression, true or not, that he has things other than his career on his mind, consequently that he might prefer being in the audience to being on stage, might prefer passivity to pathos, blankness to the clever turn, and that he might very well, without trying to romanticize it, entertain an art that is resistant to his sympathy. In "Expression," he flees the literary exercises of his suffering students and goes to stand in a museum before an early Italian altarpiece whose Christchild is knowing, massive, composed, and alien: "The sight quenches, like water / after too much birthday cake." Throughout his new volume, the poet does a very fine job of interpreting closed realms, whether the realm is religious painting, animals (in this book it's cats), a rock star, a transvestite, or a sluggish young cousin. Toward all these "foreign powers," the poet conducts himself with generosity; he is not wounding, only judging.

This is, then, poetry responsive to cultivation not of the ground but of the faculty for attention and discernment in the self. Although Thom Gunn plays down the overt allegory and literary machinery as much as Wendell Berry, unlike Berry he has little interest in literal symbol and natural metonymy, and would rather locate the most lucid and colloquial metaphor for the network he is constructing. The rough gravel of the daylight world in the following lines from "Slow Waker" also implicates adult challenge and adult callus ahead for the unformed, aimless adolescent cousin, caught "between the flow of night, / ceaselessly braiding itself, / and the gravelly beach / that our soles have thickened on." The test of a good poem therefore is not how well it disappears before the phenomena, but how crucial a testimony it is to the very existence of the phenomena it has helped to bring to light.

This is true even when the metaphor is as quiet as "terraced" in the description of the friend's apartment he lets himself into after being out all night: "[T]he sun / ordering the untidy kitchen, / even the terraced black circles / in the worn enamel are bright." Gunn has worked up a remarkable talent for addressing the object. On the other hand, when the "object" is already more spiritualized by memory and attachment, as is true for the wind that presses the glum little lake near where he grew up, the metaphor will necessarily be more vocal. The wind in "The Exercise" helps him emerge from his own adolescent uncertainty by calling up a stalwart response: "The boisterous presence rummaged / at large in the wood . . . it was not impulse. / If I was formed by it, I was formed / by the exercise it gave me. / Exercise in stance, and / in the muscle of feeling." The seams and dowels are here meant to be visible and give pleasure by their patent artifice, as symptoms of the attentive will: "I became robust standing against it, / as I breathed it so gladly." In fact, the collaboration of the poet in framing this comparison between bodybuilding and soul making is conditioned by the experience of which he writes. The metaphor is thus compounded for the making of the poet's soul from the layman's soul: "The wind blew against me till / I tingled with knowledge. / The swiftly changing / played upon the slowly changing."

There are numerous other proofs of Thom Gunn's metaphorical range, which I wish I could quote—the old intellectual's self-willed position as a piece of orbiting flotsam in "Crosswords"; the painter's preparatory brooding that takes the form of weight lifting, which the poet compares to a hitchhiker's adjustment of his knapsack as he wanders a road that in turn appears as a central serpentine shape in one of his paintings ("Selves"); or the comic "anatomy" of the child's world in "Hide and Seek," with its universe of offspring (the moon among them) hugging their mothers. In a slightly different vein, the dramatic monologue of the night taxi driver is an artifice of breathtaking control. But I will quote from only one last work, the clear triumph of *The Passages of Joy*, the five-section "Talbot Road," a tribute to a handsome heterosexual friend now dead (Tony) by the homosexual poet-speaker. In the mid-sixties, when he again had lived in London, the poet's persona could see from his "excellent room" in Talbot Road his friend in another room some blocks away working at translations. In poems two and three, Gunn separately explores the loneliness of Tony—so adored, so used to tributes—and the loneliness of his own youth. Then in the fourth poem, shortly before leaving to return to the States, he is given a party by Tony on a boat on the Thames, which suddenly reveals the open secrets they had all their lives just glimpsed—the craft of the self now buoyant, as Thom Gunn's identity is, on the stream of sexuality, time, instinct, and young life:

> The party slipped
> through the watery network of London,
> grid that had always been glimpsed
> out of the corner of the eye
> behind fences or from the tops of buses.
> Now here we were, buoyant on it,
> picnicking, gazing in mid-mouthful
> at the backs of buildings, at smoke-black walls
> coral in the light of the long evening,
> at what we had suspected all along
> when we crossed the bridges we now passed under,
> gliding through the open secret.

When, in the last poem of the "Talbot Road" sequence, the speaker returns fifteen years later to a changed scene, he remembers one final manifestation of this long, sweet stream. In 1965, in the building across the way, he could see a young man who was perhaps visiting a relative in town; he looked "country," intent, fresh, alert, gazing down at the street, at "that fine public flow at the edge of which / he waited, poised, detached in wonder / and in no hurry / before he got ready one day / to climb down into its live current." The boy is one of those "closed realms" so impeccably touched out by a Gunn cameo. The metaphor of the future as a current is at once moving and economical, almost literal. Marvelously, the river of time seems new and just, because Thom Gunn has made it personal to himself. For the boy's preparations to climb down into the live current hold, in an overt figure of abundance, nerve, and promise, a shadow-figure of relinquishment—an utterly different sort of release, as the poet allows his friend, and his own past, to sink down and be carried beyond him out of sight.

# From "Outsiders"

Les A. Murray's *Vernacular Republic* is an introduction to an alien country (Australia) through the medium of an English that is not American, not British, not a dialect like the "nation language" of Edward Kamau Brathwaite or the patois of Derek Walcott, and not an overtly adversarial language like the Anglo-Saxon attitudes of Seamus Heaney. Because the "vernacular" of Mr. Murray's title means more than the colloquial or spoken language distinguished from the literary or written, his "republic" is less narrow than the territory staked out by the colonial. The root of "vernacular," the Latin *verna*, meant a slave born in his master's house, hence in adjectival form "vernacular" came to define the condition of being bound to place with double ties, those of external coercion as well as those of blood and memory. In the case of Les A. Murray, son of farmers of Welsh extraction, the double ties are the more cunningly interwoven as the coercive element loosens into willingness. The poet defines his territory not by wresting it from the Crown but by addressing, with a whole heart, the peculiar and forbidding landscapes, the odd layerings of the light, and the savage contrasts between seasons and elevations in his home region of New South Wales.

Murray is concerned with the profound human isolation of the widely scattered farms of the plateaus and the logging

Review of Les A. Murray, *The Vernacular Republic: Selected Poems* (New York: Persea Books, 1982); Dick Davis, *Seeing the World* (London: Anvil Press, 1980); Alan Stephens, *In Plain Air: Poems 1958–1980* (Athens, Ohio: Swallow Press, 1982); Herbert Morris, *Peru* (New York: Harper & Row, 1983).

camps of the high, cool country. One is reminded of the daunting face of the early American frontier, yet as soon as we put ours alongside the Australian's, we realize, with a shock, how much less somber and maniac Murray's vision is than that of our fathers. Driving through small sawmill towns (the romance of the auto as common there as here), the speaker of one exuberant poem slows down physically and perceptually as he leaves the forest. He enters the "bare hamlets" punctuated at their far ends by "a little sidelong creek alive with pebbles" (the momentum of the driver is still alive in the current of that description). Then, much more slowly, he passes the sawmill itself:

> The mills are roofed with iron, have no walls:
> you look straight in as you pass, see lithe men working,
> the swerve of a winch,
> dim dazzling blades advancing
> through a trolley-borne trunk
> till it sags apart
> in a manifold sprawl of weatherboards and battens.
> ("Driving Through Sawmill Towns")

The prying open of boards by the huge blade is at once cumbrous (as is the gawking of the driver) and clean (as is the shyness of the mill hands who watch him): "The men watch you pass: / when you stop your car and ask them for directions, / tall youths look away— / it is the older men who / come out in blue singlets and talk softly to you. // Beside each mill, smoke trickles out of mounds / of ash and sawdust" ("Driving Through Sawmill Towns"). There is real mastery in that last turn toward the object—not the tragic diction of Frost's "Woodpile" ("the slow smokeless burning of decay"), but a grace note given out before the next section, which begins, "You glide on through town, / your mudguards damp with cloud."

These passages of human contact and soft exchange sediment the poems as they proceed, basing feeling in place, so that the poet can negotiate between the lyric and the letter of the work with no sense of strain. The literal machinery of journey and setting in *The Vernacular Republic* increasingly opens to response. Most of the strong poems here are descriptive. Few are simple in diction, although the exceptions are instructive: "I walk about. The silo, tall as Time / casts on bright straws its coldly southward shade" ("Troop Train Returning"). More commonly, however, the diction is complex, interwoven, and exhilarating, as if not only the world but also the language were being flushed, shaken, then drawn fresh-side-out. "The Grassfire Stanzas" show a farmer burning dead grass to clear the way for the new green leaves already growing underneath:

> Fretted with small flame, the aspiring islands leave
> off plumes behind. Smuts shower up every thermal
> to float down long stairs. Aggregate smoke attracts a kestrel.
> . . . . . . . . . . . . . . . . . . . . . . . . . . . . . . . . . . . . . . . . . . . . . . .
> The green feed that shelters beneath its taller death yearly
> is unharmed, under new loaf soot. Arriving hawks teeter
> and plunge continually, working over the hopping outskirts.

With what relish does the poet pinpoint his lexical inventions, deploying the nicely energetic vowels among rugged consonants. Then, two-thirds through the poem, the metaphoric subtext flares up as the birds borne aloft on the heat from the fire rise to a little expressive climax (the farmer all the while mutely ordinary):

> The man carries smoke wrapped in bark, and keeps apply-
>     ing it
> starting the new circles. He is burning the passive ocean
> around his ark of buildings and his lifeboat water;
>
> it wasn't this man, but it was man, sing the agile
> exclamatory birds, who taught them this rapt hunting
> (strike! in the updrafts, snap! of hardwood pods).
> Humans found the fire here. It is inherent. They learn,
> wave after wave of them, how to touch the country.
>
> ("The Grassfire Stanzas")

It is likewise the poet's goal to learn "how to touch the country," to express without exploiting, to burn without killing—yet, decidedly, to burn.

The poet is not always successful. Several tendencies mar the book. One is a bullyboy cleverness that feeds on shock, sometimes of a fairly juvenile variety ("the day kids began smoking the armpit hairs of wisdom"). A second unhappy tendency is toward the fashionable primitive. "The Buladelah-Taree Holiday Song Cycle" is an attempt to imitate one of the aborigine song cycles, and Murray shows again here how arresting his descriptive diction can be. But the effect of his nine-page cycle is at once aimless and punishing. Here is a plenty so dense and continuous as to grow, gradually, uniform:

> Abandoned fruit trees, moss-tufted, spotted with dim lichen
> paints; the fruit trees of the Grandmothers
> . . . . . . . . . . . . . . . . . . . . . . . . . . . . . . . . . . .
> the fruit has the taste of former lives, of sawdust and parlour
> song, the tang of Manners:
> children bite it, recklessly,
> at what will become for them the place of the Slab Wall and
> of the Coal Oil Lamp,
> the place of moss-grit and swallows' nests, the place of the
> Crockery.

These last lines remind us how difficult it is to fit modern things into primitive phrase: The result is oracular pidgin.

Les A. Murray is far more successful when he turns toward opinion and idea. He is fond of the generous Horatian meditation interleaved with wit and sensibility—a kind of poem whose most famous modern genius was W. H. Auden; a kind of poem that has also been practiced, with more savagery, by Murray's older compatriot, A. D. Hope. Murray, if not exactly rougher than either one, is somewhat more urgent and rapid. His most charming effort in the vein of wit and urbanity is "Quintets for Robert Morley," a poem about the advantages of being fat:

> We were probably the earliest
> civilized, and civilizing, humans,
> the first to win the leisure,
> sweet boredom, life-enhancing sprawl
> that require style.
> . . . . . . . . . . . . . . . . . .

We were the first moderns
after all, being like the Common Man
disqualified from tragedy.
. . . . . . . . . . . . . . . . .
Never trust a lean meritocracy
nor the leader who has been lean;
only the lifelong big have the knack of wedding
greatness with balance.

In "First Essay on Interest" and "Equanimity," Murray is addressing subjects that already command our agreement; we all grant that even-temperedness and a mild vivacity of address are virtues. The poet's task, then, is clearly to move from the single virtues narrowly construed to the multiply virtuous life—to press the one quality into its transition states with the many others that the good man must hold in cooperative suspension. The poem must also convince us that pleasure and restraint are interdependent. I think Murray does this when he imagines the body riding downhill on a bike as one ages, when "interest retreats from the face":

it becomes a vivid steady state
that registers every grass-blade seen on the way,
the long combed grain in the steps, free insects flying;
it stands aside from your panic, the wracked disarray;
it behaves as if it were the part of you not dying.
("First Essay on Interest")

And in an Australia that is no Arcadia, all he can hope for is the equanimity that serves to make men tolerant and mild:

Almost beneath notice, as attainable as gravity, it is
a continuous hovering moment. Pity the high madness
that misses it continually, ranging without rest between
assertion and unconsciousness,
the sort that makes hell seem a height of evolution.
("Equanimity")

Instead of grief, vengeance, and passion (those advanced but hellish eruptions), we are shown by equanimity how to avoid "being trapped in the point"; this flexible state is compared to "a field all foreground, and equally all background, / like a painting of equality. Of infinite detailed extent / like God's attention. Where nothing is diminished by perspective."

The next group of poets all give significant amounts of space to this area of human experience so aptly characterized by Les A. Murray in "Equanimity" as the "quiet air between the bars of our attention," a state of individual bliss like that available even to the minor figures in religious painting before Masaccio, "Where nothing is diminished by perspective." That is to say that Dick Davis and Alan Stephens, and to a lesser extent Herbert Morris, are all paying homage to classical poetic virtues like measure and restraint, and to postures like sociable inwardness, which give the poets so much flexibility in choosing their topics and taking in material. Dick Davis and Alan Stephens are especially conscious of working in styles that measure the verse line, and they often rhyme. Hence we will hear in them a much sharper phrasing of idea than we heard in Les Murray's work.

Dick Davis is one of those poets who seems to have been born into the wrong period. My first impulse is to place him in the eighteenth century, but he would be as quickly swallowed up and forgotten by the audience for mock epic and Juvenalian satire as he appears to be now by the current audience for unchecked associationism and unabashed ego. Nor does the High Renaissance offer Davis a niche; unlike the many writers of epigrams and epigrammatic lyrics then, who also wrote plays and masques and sonnet cycles and satires and elegies and verse epistles and songs and philosophical meditations, British poet Dick Davis writes epigrams and epigrammatic lyrics, period. He is thus in secondary shadow wherever one places him—not so much doomed as designed to be an antidote to what current fashion indulges.

Viewed in this light, Davis's small world is perfect, but cramped, and many of his most exquisite poems fall automatically into postures of moody pessimism and cold rigor. These are, very clearly, artifacts, inventions, *made things*, rather than the expressions of congenial and accustomed roles. In the fine poem "Winter," the awkward, dated jargon of the cognitivist, "inapprehensible," continues to perch outside the body of the poem, just as "quotidian" makes an overdeliberate gesture of assent toward middle-aged abstraction. In the shade of these two anomalies, "Winter's" other milder verbal attitudes (a quizzical passivity; blank openness to depression, loneliness, and insult) seem a little bit less genuine, for all their precision. Of course, the merely descriptive poet has a much easier time of it, for all he asks of details is that they diffuse like a mist in the direction of general psychology. Davis's kind of work is much more courageous and precarious, because he attempts to speak from the psychological state toward the supporting detail:

*Winter*

Your moment comes, inapprehensible.
Autumnal cold pervades the mountain pool;
The tense, still surface glistens; it is ice.
I peer, but cannot see what lives or dies.

Quotidian despair, I feel your cold lips
Searching me in the dark, your soft hand grips
With an enormous strength: I tremble, yours.
It is your hand that guides me now, explores

The vacant world for me.
              I walk at night,
Possessed by the cold: on a building-site
Smoke from the watchman's fire smarts in my eyes:
Brief greetings clash, like gravel thrown on ice.

Despite my reservations about diction, I am more deeply taken with the poem "Winter" each time I read it. The surface of the mountain pool imperceptibly thickens its surface into ice as line 3 moves to its climax at the semicolon. The second stanza directs us toward an erotic encounter with the succubus despair, yet just at the end of the stanza, at line 8, when the speaker is about to swoon under its dark caress, the line enjambs and he is cast out into severer cold, stumbling a bit at the broken ninth line and, thereafter, on the gravel and icy debris around the deserted building site. By this third stanza in the poem, after we have admired the poetical mountain pool and accepted the unrealistic grappling with a personified emotion, we trust the poet's control of the metaphoric. Thus to meet a "vacant world" filled with naturalistic props (the excavation; a trash fire in a drum) confirms and concentrates the poem from a new angle, adding a fearful urban plot to analogies by which first nature and then the psyche of the speaker had been introduced.

Now the world of the ugly, gritty, meager, and contingent city looms before the desperate man. There is no healing warmth, no human comfort here. Furthermore, the simile "like gravel thrown on ice" reminds us that when the speaker peered through the ice on the mountain pool, he'd been unable to see any creature there in *any* state: So at the poem's end are all the creatures cased in ice, the greetings they summon clashing against those obscure and hardened vacancies. The poem is brilliantly controlled; it is also utterly grim.

The mode Davis excels in requires a calculated distance from experience, a clean passivity where personality is concerned; but finally the unanticipated goal of empathy and participation in the fearful is reached. The fact that the goal is feeling insures the lyrical foundation, while the passivity insures that the poem will also reflect upon what it feels. Such a double role is at the very heart of metaphor, for unless they stand at some distance from the vortex, poets have no perspective from which to abstract, while without a vortex (and the seizure and chaos it imposes), there is no core. To make metaphor, one must stand in both places simultaneously—outside the sufferer, where pain and craving are always twofold, and inside the experience, where there is no distinction to be made between the person and the feeling, so that one cannot even separate out a noun like "sufferer" from the state that is all self, all need:

*Dying*

Illness, and prayer.
From the window
Darkness: his stare
On the dark snow.

The nurse: in her
Hands reality,
A glinting blur—
A certainty.

Prayer and dark snow.
The nurse recedes.
She is real, though
Not what he needs.

Davis deftly interweaves the dimeter lines with the rhymes
that try to cut them off and with the longer units of syntax
that try to open them out again. He strains the fabric at one
point only, when he hovers over the enjambment in the penul-
timate line so that two meanings jostle each other for a
moment—(a) the assertion that the nurse is more real than
the morphine she administers (as if the line had the emphasis,
"*She* is real, though"); and (b) the more circumspect knowl-
edge that her reality is irrelevant ("She is real, though not
what he needs"). The moment at which the two meanings
overlap is very brief, very guarded, and very minor; it is from
these qualities of modesty and economy that many of Dick
Davis's poems derive their small, fierce pathos.

Within the plain style, Alan Stephens writes a more voluble
sort of poem. For one thing, he does not constrain his poetry
as Dick Davis does to weigh the furthest things under the
severest circumstances. The title of Stephens's selected po-
ems, *In Plain Air*, with its pun on the French for "outdoors,"
"in the open," *en plein air*, points both to the transparency of
the poet's landscapes and to the slight thickness of his humor.
The book has too many superior poems to list, let alone dis-
cuss; what is more tantalizing than their number, however, is
the variety of modes, traditions, and voices Alan Stephens has
mastered over the years.

He has outgrown several striking apprenticeships, one to
Yvor Winters ("Moments in a Glade"), one to Marianne
Moore ("The Dragon of Things"), and he appears to have
attached himself for a time (of all models!) to the prose tales
of Ernest Hemingway ("Memorial Bronze"). In that work of
Stephens's not markedly indebted to any obvious literary pres-

ences, however, a native genius for descriptive meditation stands out. It is a clearer and less rhapsodic gift then Les A. Murray's, and hence can move us by gentler plays of sound. In the following passage we encounter huge stumps of logs (each weighing tons), tumbled and left by a logging company at a bend in a river, the bark stripped by time and weather until they are silvery white. Note the low, heavy thud of short *u* and broad *o* and the consonant cognates *d/t* and *p/b*: "now in their casual magnitude / and stillness they seem of the gods, / seem like the white bulls of a god / driven into this place between cliffs / and sea, and possessing it / now in the repose of their might" ("The Green Cape"). The mythic allusion is clear but nonspecific: Any general recollection of the sacrifices in Homer will suffice to key the scene. The very vagueness of reference is part of the poignancy of the metaphor, inasmuch as the gods to whom the white bulls were dear have been forgotten, worn away by time; one recollects this fact with a start, just as one might be startled on first seeing all those gleaming white trunks warping in the river. The dereliction of the loggers is like our neglect of homage to those who made us.

A moral dimension characteristically emerges from Alan Stephens's realistic descriptions. The sparse fungi and lichens of the Arctic (some grow for only one day in the whole year) fasten to anything, rock, bone, antler, "in the long / darkness each bright patch / holding fast to its object." And that is the end of this short free-verse poem. But "bright patch" persists like an afterimage; the bright moss continues to propagate itself by its loyal adherence to another thing.

I think the suggestibility of this and other free-verse poems by Stephens is owing to the fact that he turns from syllabics and accentual-syllabic poems to free-verse when he wants to look with a certain hushed realism at the world of his desire. That is to say, this is free verse by a poet to whom many other modes are also available. The free verse thus has a purity and an inevitability:

> . . . and then the air going
> gray green with the rain

clattering suddenly,
water bunched, quivering,
dragged by the heavy wind
in long diagonal welts
across the old window,
as if the glass were melting—
as it is, in fact, the panes
being thicker at the bottom,
ever so slightly,
after all these years, from the slow
downward pour of the glass

("The Window: In Time of Drought")

*In Plain Air* has two long poems that polarize the book. One, about the plains, "Tree Meditation," is a 260-line poem in seven-syllable lines, which uses all the syllabic poem's resources of rhythmical asymmetry and conversational syntax. The tree is the huge cottonwood usually found wherever a river, stream, or ditch runs. Stephens explores philosophical reveries as well as the mundane life suggested by the tree's cycle. Occasionally, when the reverie has been well handled, the mundane observations assume more profound scope. There are also little digressions and subplots that come into play, sometimes mild, like a breeze pouring through the entire tree, which seem to Stephens like "the musings of the tree." Once, a funeral passes: "I feel / like waving to them, but check / the impulse." Recently, he had seen cottonwoods being felled and the fallen "sections of the trunks / and limbs [looked] like fallen big game / in Africa—great females / slain and strewn about." Most important, he remembers a dream that came to him as a child the magical number of times (three). There is a giant poplar with a seeping gall like a mossy green hump from which pure water trickled. When he goes up to it, "a cavern / slopes upward into the huge / interior of the tree" and there in the cave mouth stands a great deer:

according to the dream's plan
I've had a look at my life,
which is all I was to do—
this was the feeling at first;

then the sense of the dream changed—
the deer was merely life
itself being presented
in repose for a moment
so that I could look at it.

("Tree Meditation")

I am impressed by how clearly and modestly the poet is able to substitute deep meanings, to correct his own favored dream-readings. Further, I believe the verbal assignments of "presentation" by the deer and receptivity in the dreamer, and find them convincing—revealing, as they do, a certain satisfaction in temporary repose.

The second large work is the sequence of seventy-two Petrarchan sonnets, "Running at Hendry's." As the writer forewarns us, the individual poems are often less telling than are clusters and suites of poems. "The old sonnet sequences [presumably those of Spenser, Sidney, Shakespeare, and their contemporaries] . . . take up as no single poem can the unpredictable mix of experiences and themes with the prevailing passion, all going on during a longish stretch of time." Mr. Stephens, who teaches literature at Santa Barbara, knows well how to disarm the reader. The sonnets *are* flawed, but in a way that, he suggests, the author of the *Amoretti* might approve:

Then there are the scraps of narrative that come out incidentally, the shifts (alas) in the passion itself, the sense that each poem is being done at a sitting with the time passing, that an idea that doesn't come through satisfactorily here may turn up later (only now with a fresh secondary theme jostling it which later becomes itself a main theme), the untidy couplings of metaphysics and peevishness, jealousy or other unworthy emotions, this or that unrelated preoccupation obtruding along the way, the speaker himself changing willy-nilly, the bits of news, glooms, dull stretches, elations—and the old types, the anniversary sonnet, the insomniac sonnet, the sonnet about the sonnet. (Note to "Running at Hendry's")

I can't imagine saying it better. Obtrusions, untidiness, bits of things, stretches that lead nowhere and take forever, obligatory subjects—all occur as distractions in the career of any poet; but according to the postromantic outlook, which we all find in some way convincing, all these distractions have a definite value in irking, goading, or exploding the poem into its proper, final fire. Thus the oddments in this sequence of sonnets are almost welcomed by the author as proof both of his unpresumptuous desire for literary exercise and of his ability to knit something out of his life's very randomness. But like the blank sonnets in Robert Lowell's *History*, these poems are very much five-finger exercises in which certain traits (here, boyishness and self-dramatization) are exaggerated.

Among the many dazzling passages of description in "Running at Hendry's," I am most fond of those about the taut, wet surface of the sand; those that describe moonrise and the way the moon skims alongside him in the water on his return run; the descriptions of storm light at the horizon; of the herons, gulls, pelicans, and sanderlings "like so much scrap-iron hurled in the air"; and of the black stumplike bodies of the surfers in wetsuits, waiting in the troughs for the last right wave to take them in. I will quote one sonnet that, like at least a dozen of the Hendry's Beach suite, moves beyond description a little ways to show us not just life in motion but also experience in flux:

### Noon Swimmers, Plovers, a Young Heron, a Grebe

People are black on silver this mid-day
Far up the beach, the waves withdrawing show
Light rustling in the grit, the plovers throw
Shadows appearing solider than they,
And the young heron that lives here flaps away
And alights up ahead in the backflow
That glares more silver as it slips below
The nubs of the bright foam, the sunny spray,
While the grebe I come on has been lying dead,
At the water's edge, on his back. His wings are spread
As if in flight. He looks heraldic, too—
Like the scrawny phoenix D. H. Lawrence drew.
But this bird's missing an eye; bedraggled and sad
Lies here for a little the only self he had.

(#63 of "Running at Hendry's")

Although the syntax would show continuity of statement from line one through line ten, there is a definite turn of theme right where one expects it in a sonnet of this type, after line eight. Subtle shifts in rhythm throughout the basically regular pentameter (even the highly irregular sixth line) provide background for the increasingly dramatic rhythms that come in the sestet, rhythms which in turn support the argument that, although this was not an important death, the grebe's slight self receives the homage of precise attention. The whole sequence is intelligent, professional, and easygoing, and makes me look forward to the poems Stephens will continue to draw from his enormous poetic reserve.

Herbert Morris writes in smooth and hypnotic monotones. He composes by means of a twofold prosodic device played carefully against a simple rhetorical device. Morris uses alternating stresses and slacks—although, unlike most metrical poets, he chooses falling rather than rising rhythm, so that, particularly in the tetrameter line, these trochaic feet will inevitably echo *Hiawatha*:

> Stepping deftly to the jetty,
> members of the boating party
> . . . . . . . . . . . . . . . . . . . . . . .
> walk the ramp to the misty shore.
> The sand is grey, the water greyer,
> the light a queasy off-grey color
> depriving everything of shadow.
>
> ("Newport, 1930")

Even in pentameter lines, the light endings will recall to many readers Henry Wadsworth Longfellow's attempt to make the English trochaic line into a bardic meter.

Another feature of the prosody here is that syntax in Morris's poems tends to coincide with the line, creating multiple series of recurrent and homogeneous lines:

> The sticks were tapered, long, immensely graceful.
> . . . . . . . . . . . . . . . . . . . . . . . . . . . . . . . . . . . . . .
> These whittled spears, these decorated slivers
> . . . . . . . . . . . . . . . . . . . . . . . . . . . . . . . . . . .

his speech would falter, his complexion darken.

. . . . . . . . . . . . . . . . . . . . . . . . . . . . . . . . . . .

When words of ivory chopsticks reached the Viscount

. . . . . . . . . . . . . . . . . . . . . . . . . . . . . . . . . . . . . .

The sea, in China, was of great importance

("History of China")

The prosodic characteristics that create a droning effect find support in the serial method of narration, flat statements ranked one upon another with only slight variations from one appearance to the next. Like many demanding French forms, Morris's fairly rigid framework permits only a small movement away from the first predication. In fact, the model his narrative method most resembles is the pantoum, the Malayan schema for verbatim repetition of entire lines in endless successions of quatrains (*ABAB BCBC,* where the letters represent whole lines rather than merely end-rhymes). Interestingly, the pantoum requires the development of different themes in the neighboring pairs of lines, thus making legal and correct the willful thematic distortion of each line, made to serve two masters.

The repeating lines and phrases in Morris (occurring as what I call would "tags") are not manipulated in such rigid contradiction, yet each time a tag-phrase or tag-line recurs, it is as if it had, since its last appearance, been honeycombed with new irony, new weariness, new vistas of disappointed longing. He exploits the fact (known to Robbe-Grillet and other experimental artists) that, even when minor, detail can be made ominously significant by its recurrence against a background from which all ordinarily significant events have been barred. Of course, the small detail will naturally be more menacing when the background—which may lack local intricacy of thought or the texture of exchange—nevertheless implicates, as it does in "At the Château de Villegenis That Summer," massive upheaval of men and minds.

"That Summer," the epigraph tells us, is September, 1918. We are slightly southwest of Paris at the estate of W. E. Corey. We are looking at a picture of "Mrs. W. E. Corey playing cards with the wounded officers. . . . Mrs. Corey, or Mabelle Gilman, an actress, was the wife of the president of Carnegie Steel Company and United States Steel." Against the grander backdrop (supplied by the caption's stark contrast between American money and metal and European dead), between *our* nouveau riche and *their* longstanding culture, Morris can afford to be arch and noncommittal about the real issues: "Perhaps it is the drama of her hat / in contrast to the bare heads of the soldiers, / heads made by half-light even more austere, / which proves, for all this radiance, unsettling: / Italian lattice-work trimmed with organza." Mrs. Corey (alias Mabelle Gilman) will brook no hint of unpleasantness, even though the very idea of playing whist with wounded officers invites a whiff of unmentionable suffering, for suddenly, "in the heat of the bidding,"

> a head nods, or a hand begins to quiver,
> an arm, quite inexplicably, goes numb,
> a breeze stirs in the willow, a leg twitches,
>
> fever flushes a cheek, the body trembles,
> perspiration assails a lip, a palm,
> or the gaze wanders off to a bird scrawling
> passionate, living signs across a sky
> too blinding, too immense, to be searched further.

The poet here suggests the collective recoil from reality, although he makes it clear that behind the cultural implication (that modern war, like modern metal, money, and power, is too immensely dazing to be searched further) there lies the more immediate physical one (head wounds, amputations, incisions, mustard gas burns, shellshock—these drive the mind of the soldier inward, away from the "signs").

Finally, what Herbert Morris's method can permit him is the passionate concentration on a hurt that his persona does not yet quite comprehend. As if the serial rhetoric had, in its casting-up of the random nugget, presented to the perambulating consciousness its own sullen emblem, personal but also encoded and speechless, the narrator worries at the "secret" of the wristwatch protruding from one wounded officer's overlarge sleeve. Tag-phrases long since introduced and recurring here include the serving of tea and the falling of light and fragrance from the whist players. "Steel" brings us back to the factories of W. E. Corey:

> One soldier rests a small hand on his thigh.
> A watch strapped to the wrist looms from a shirtcuff
> not quite long enough to insure concealment.
> Here, at once, from the moment you first see it,
> here, from this pale-eyed man's ill-fitting shirt,
>
> its sleeve not covering all a sleeve covers,
> here, with this steel chronometer whose hands
> seem suddenly too heavy, too explicit,
> the numbers staring from the face too bold,
> the sun striking crystal cold, too cold,
>
> tea served, or not served, cakes passed, never passed,
> beyond, late summer fragrance in the trees,
> you have the thing you need, or think you need;
> you know all injury must lie with that;
> you touch the wound, intact: time passed, time passing.
>
> ("At the Château de Villegenis That Summer")

Certainly, something of this officer's own sense of the fatuity of tea and cakes in light of what he knows comes through here. So does the narrator's burgeoning horror at the long vanished past, and at the amputation of all knowledge and all effort: The wound is time. This poem is a powerful evocation of the modern age as a roll call of unforgivable and unredeemable acts, the poem itself riskily imitating the oblivion of its actors in its mechanical seriality and in the barrage of redundant details, which are also the screens behind which reason can shrink.

# From "Pictures from Borges"

*"There are infinite things on earth; any one of them may be
likened to any other."*

—*Jorge Luis Borges*

The work of Anglo-Welsh poet Gillian Clarke is serious, delicate, and on the whole, wonderfully fresh. She is both a poet of place and a painter of psychological landscapes, and those points at which portrait and projection merge are often disturbing in their power. *Letter from a Far Country* is a volume of meditations on the solitudes that penetrate and surround domestic existence in a rural village. The poet's method is associative, and although association may be said to have its own logic, it is perhaps not various and coherent enough by itself to organize an entire poetics. It may be that the adjustment of surfaces to show symbolic layering, albeit interesting, is both arbitrary and microscopic—abstract at the small end of the scale. This is Clarke's limitation; working against it, she gives pleasure by her acute and sensitive observation and (more crucial traits) by her good sense and tact.

In her title poem Gillian Clarke is abstract in another and more expansive sense, for she assumes as primary the woman's obligation (corroborated in all the ballads where the minstrel boy leaves the maid behind) to pass the time while she stays put. Because "There's always been time on our hands," acts of reverie, such as sea-gazing, are bound to feel very different for the women of the countryside than for the

---

Review of Gillian Clarke, *Letter from a Far Country* (Manchester: Carcanet New Press, 1982); James Reiss, *Express* (Pittsburgh: University of Pittsburgh Press, 1983); Derek Mahon, *The Hunt by Night* (Winston-Salem: Wake Forest University Press, 1982).

men of whom the world makes outwardly more strenuous demands. Not only is the hilly coastal country of Wales ancestral, it is for Clarke "essentially feminine," by which the author reminds us that this is a history—loose, episodic, impressionistic—of the women in her family and parish, who practiced the housewifely tasks required by the men who worked the fields and mines. And although at many points in the past, as the following passage suggests, craft and culture, distaff and plough, were nominally balanced, the poet permits the deepest reverberations of the heart to commend the former, while the relation between the sexes is subtly torn by the imagery of mill-blade, shuttle, beak, and knife that trouble the domestic weave. A hundred years ago: "Water-wheels milled the sunlight / and the loom's knock was a heart / behind all activity. / The shuttles were quick as birds / in the warp of oakwoods. / In the fields the knives were out / in a glint of husbandry."

The quick birds to which the moving shuttles are compared exist, naturalistically, outside the comparison as well: They are the tutelary spirits of the women in cottages who yearn for the open air and open road, yet are intimidated by the risk of something that haunts their yearning from the other side of its satisfaction:

> From the opposite wood the birds
> ring like a tambourine. It's not
> the birdsong of a garden, thrush
> and blackbird, robin and finch,
> distinguishable, taking turns.
> The song's lost in saps and seepings,
> amplified by hollow trees,
> cupped leaves and wind in the branches.

In this, the darkening labyrinth of the folk tale, the birds cannot sing clearly enough for us to distinguish them; their messages—their very species—are lost in echoes, dampened by leaf mold and forest decay. This haunting sense of meaning lost and confounded, of fibers and family traits subtly broken down, of emptiness that may once have been actual conversation, suggests a negative outcome for restless desire. Yearning is fulfilled not in freedom but in enchantment, a state bewitched and hollow whose music is a wild tambourine, an indistinguishable jangling.

Not all of the female figures are at the same pitch of discontent; some are creatures of willing domesticity. While recognizing the cost in thought and inwardness of a life thus devoted, Clarke respects this motive, recognizing even in herself the urge to launder, fold, label, measure, and make. But the associational contours of her home-thoughts are aligned with the hive, the field, the sea, and the gemstone in such a way that claustrophobia is delayed: "The chests and cupboards are full, / the house sweet as a honeycomb. / I move in and out of the hive / all day, harvesting, ordering"; "the saucers of marmalade / are set when the amber wrinkles / like the sea if you blow it." One feels, in the ripple of graceful imagining in these examples, a large opening of horizons.

But poverty, isolation, or unguessed-at fear and rage drive others to the brink. In the forceful memoir "Llyr," the young protagonist connects language to the betrayals to come. The poem, naturally, is in blank verse, the form that so transparently registers both literary conventionality and independence. Seeing a performance of *Lear*, the speaker learns the meaning of "little words," "All. Nothing. Fond. Ingratitude." Clarke's feeling for rural Wales opens a new dimension on the play, picking up these hints of tragic sentiment between father and daughter, played out among storms and breakers:

> The landscape's marked with figures of old men:
> The bearded sea; thin-boned, wind-bent trees;
> Shepherd and labourer and night-fisherman.
> Here and there among the crumbling farms
> Are lit kitchen windows in distant hills,
> And guilty daughters longing to be gone.

The tableau presented by the daughter's cottage lights is one of many excellent uses of metaphorically resonant descriptive detail in *Letter from a Far Country*. The poems about mowing are especially deft. The hay being carted back to barns along narrow lanes gets caught in the branches, betokening a hurt to everyone who inadvertently makes this connection: "Men in the fields. / Loads following the lanes, / strands of yellow hair caught in the hedges." In a second poem, after the grain is cut down, the height of the field does indeed appear to have "fallen": "You know the hay's in / when gates hang slack / in the lanes. These hot nights / the fallen fields lie open"—again, a subtle sexual humiliation seems built into the seasons and shapes of things. In another poem, the writer recaptures something of a skaldic feeling as, driving along an industrial dump in a rough storm, she has a near-collision with a swooping heron. She calls him, quite credibly, an "archangel / come to re-open the heron-roads . . . where wind comes flashing off water / interrupting the warp of the snow / and the broken rhythms of the blood." All three are bright moments within subdued poems, but they show great flair.

In more completely realized works, it is not the radiant *aperçu* but a tougher consciousness that connects and controls, and here again, Clarke turns to other poets to frame the conditions of insight. Reading Wordsworth to a ward of mentally ill adults, she reports how a heretofore mute laborer rises to his humanity as he breaks a half-century of silence to recite with her, verbatim, from memory, "I Wandered Lonely as a Cloud" ("They flash upon that inward eye / Which is the bliss of solitude"). The occasion is risky, but the poet manages to control it: "The nurses are frozen, alert; the patients / seem to listen. He is hoarse but word-perfect. / Outside the daffodils are still as wax." In a companion poem, in the geriatric ward, an old woman with a young mind mesmerizes the speaker, who is reading from *The Merchant of Venice*. The gentle, undiscriminating rain, of course, ironically links the famous speech of Portia ("The quality of mercy is not strained; / It droppeth as the gentle rain from heaven / Upon the place beneath") to the grim, bare weather of Wales, which is also (as we have heard in the *Lear* poem) the weather of age, remorse, and grief:

## Mrs Frost

Turning my head a moment
from the geriatrics' ward
I see the bare wood bowed
quietly under the rain,
mists rising in silence.

Her white head is lowered
to her one good shaking hand,
clear thoughts rising from a body
ninety-two years old and done-for,
waiting to look up, blue, blind,

from another century
when I stop reading. Portia
perfectly remembered, just
and gentle in her mind and mine
The undiscriminating rain

brisk as nurses, chills the wood
to the bones as night comes on.
In the beaded silks of rain
the trees feed secretly
while she, not sleeping, remembers.

The music of "Mrs Frost," so understated, is almost entirely a matter of assonance (long *i* in the first three stanzas, short *i* and long *e* in the last) and of short free-verse lines that tend to bracket three or four stresses together while slightly altering the rhythms (note the difference between the last two lines, both nominally three-stress: the penultimate so insistent and raw, the last so delicate and recessional). The music and diction, which emphasize in such unemphatic ways, avoid the two patent dangers of the subject, yammering and pontificating; we are given to estimate perfectly the dilemma of Mrs. Frost and thus to respect the courage of her continued mental application.

Where Gillian Clarke might suggest the attractions of a racial rather than personal history, James Reiss is all Freud: memorious sentiment, temperamental rage, filial heartache, and sibling rivalry. Where Clarke explores subtly social settings, Reiss keeps riding the New York City subways, tunneling back toward the alien cityscapes that trigger his emotion. As that last metaphor suggests, James Reiss is combative and explosive, selfish and unpredictable, mournful and mean, projecting the prototypical image of the Bad Boy. Many of the poems in *Express* get by on jazz, their rhetoric so highly pitched and the metaphors and roughly encrusted images so thickly piled one kind upon another that one frequently has the impression of a manic child sitting among the strewn wreckage of his play.

Sometimes the manic energy of method is also the poetry's subject. In a poem where a younger brother blames the older for playing "Mr. Top / Dog on the Bunk Bed, Mr. Big / Back on the High School Football Team," the younger one happens, years later, to be in a bar watching a pro football game, when suddenly a man guzzling beer is silhouetted against the TV as it "blazed red with an ad for Gillette . . . And I thought, Here is my blood brother / whose only gifts to me were kicks / in the teeth, his cast-off comic books, / and worst of all, wrapped, sharpened / for a lifetime, / the perfect razor of my rage." Reiss here convincingly builds a logic of association out of the bits and pieces of coincidence—for example, that for many men his age Gillette razor blades are linked to broadcast and, later, televised sports events, and that the most painful tensions between younger and older brothers occur when the older passes puberty and becomes strong and manly, enjoying a hormonal advantage the younger brother cannot make up for by any amount of will. The metaphor, "the perfect razor of my rage," as the gift of the older youth, who can shave, to the younger, who can't, works effectively on a number of levels to render a position of dramatic stand-off, intensified hatred, and final rejection.

As we move from poem to poem, we move from one momentous crescendo to another, from one act of verbal aggression to the next blow of metaphor. The only way for such work to end is in conflagration. The poet most artistically fulfills this expectation in the title poem, a series of family monologues throughout which metaphor is handled somewhat more restrainedly than in "Brothers," with the result that the climax rises out of a palpably different background. Reiss insinuates into the first monologue by a younger son the images he will make into the father's biographical details (he is a professional photographer). The two are in their sleeping berths on a train; the dim violet night-light will appear later in the red bulb of the darkroom. The father lies in the lower berth by the plate-glass window that resembles the lenses, plates, and glass through which the photographer peers. Words like "enveloping" look forward to the idea of "developing."

In the second monologue, the father speaks about awakening the next morning in Rochester, feeling exhilarated by his son's presence:

> when you grabbed my hand in a taxi
> and said, "Look at the Eastman Kodak buildings, Dad,"
> I felt as if I'd never seen a skyline: The mist
> from Genesee Falls rainbowed,
> and the glint off Kodak's red-brick compound
> hit me so hard I felt giddy . . .

Even as the father remembers his delight in his second son's company, he guiltily recalls turning against his firstborn as a result of his wife's devotion to the child. During an illness, remembers the father, speaking as if to the younger boy:

> I lay in an oxygen tent,
> dreaming my Brownie stills burned in their albums.
> Your brother's baby pictures curled aflame.
> His bonnet bulged, his crib and diapers crisped
> in the incandescent air.

The oedipally disputed first son, who speaks last, confirms the metaphysical nature of the father's photographic skills. He thinks of his father in the darkroom as making "darkness visible" in an "inferno of stillborn faces." And from his current vantage in Jerusalem, on the occasion of the father's funeral in America, the first son brings the imagery of the camera to its climax: "I stare west between the Suez Canal / and Italy's boot—seven thousand miles—until / I conjure your face, sky-blue in rigor mortis, / and kiss the frozen shutters of your eyelids." In singleminded fashion, the son mechanizes the father with the items of his craft. Although adult, he has kept before his mind's eye snapshots of his father, corroded by the father's retreat behind the things he did for a living, or worse, into loving gestures toward the younger boy—to all of which this speaker is still forced to respond anew with humiliated rage. This emotion is underscored by the combative place locations (the Suez, the *boot* of Italy); by the aggressive conjunction of rigor mortis and Kodacolor blue; and by the final compounding of forgiveness with condemnation ("and kiss the frozen shutters"). "Express" has all the earmarks of autobiography, but owing to the poet's interesting management of his dramatic gifts, it would be hard to say which brother's autobiography it was.

Elsewhere, however, the need for climactic resolution imposes extraordinary demands on rather ordinary experiences. Striking hyperbole becomes an end in itself. The very innovativeness Reiss practices, to the extent that it is unique to this poet, is shopworn, as Jorge Luis Borges observes about striking imagery in general. When we can say that *only* James Reiss could have imagined the sun rising over New Jersey as a junkie shooting up, "it is evidence that the image is banal." Through his philosopher Averroës, Borges continues: "The image one man can form is an image that touches no one. There are infinite things on earth; any one of them may be likened to any other."

There is a second kind of vanity involved in the creation of unique gestures and images. This is the assumption that the mere record of experience is valuable, that the diarist need exercise no particular selectivity, have no special literary expertise, attempt no censorship, and perform no revision once he or she has made the spontaneous photocopy of the immediate past. On occasion, the photocopy method coaxes writers into believing their thought is coherent; it covers illogic with a shroud of veridical event. This is the role of the claim "I wrote" in the following lines by Reiss: "Yet I wrote: 'she wore a barrette / and braided the dough she baked / in ovens that made me think of Treblinka' "—as if the fact that somebody wrote this down made what is written less ludicrous than it is by itself. Such a need for outside authorization should make writers suspect their methods.

I believe something of the same mental mechanism is at work in the plethora of contemporary dream poems, which, like Reiss's "Orange Ice" and "Passage," sometimes share with the diary poem only the meager justification of the circumstantial, as if to say *I really dreamed this* made the recital meritorious. But even the haunting dream is not necessarily grist for a poem, until the writer understands that non sequiturs and tableaux and the speechless omen are the terms and vocabulary of *all* dreaming, and not an explanation, rendering, or translation into art of what was dreamed in a particular case. The poet must go beyond the given—beyond even the familiar dream emotion of givenness—before the resulting poem-copy is more than a set of working notes.

Nor will shifting from sleeping vision to mystical waking vision, while easy enough to do, solve the problem:

> Ah, Conch Shell, your single note, Om,
> recalls a day in Mexico when I went walking
> on a beach and bought a conch shell from a street vendor
> and brought it back to my hotel
> balcony and blew, thinking:
> Here I am at the Pacific above brown-skinned swimmers.
> Then I felt a sudden tremor, a shock
> of incense and rosewater,
> and saw, laid out before me like a postcard,
> ten thousand pilgrims bathing in the Ganges.

This is the twelfth and final section of Reiss's "Passages," a long poem that attempts to merge the mystical with the commonplace, the eternal spirit with the shopping mall. The endeavor has a kind of absurd charm, but also a suggestion of the automatic. Any writer can drum up such a series of idly appealing claims, for example: *One quiet evening, over chop suey, I thought, "The sky is salmon pink." Then at once I heard the slicing winds of Nepal and saw a* chela *wreathed in the rainbow of his prayers.* After a while, the effect of such extrapolations is anything but whimsical; again, the self-importance of the autobiographer deadens the absurd by taking the reporting of facts as a primary good. About this shirking of a poet's chief task, Borges's Immortal speaks as follows:

> After a year's time, I have inspected these pages. I am certain they reflect the truth, but in the first chapters, and even in certain paragraphs of the others, I seem to perceive something false. This is perhaps produced by the abuse of circumstantial details, a procedure I learned from the poets and which contaminates everything with falsity, since those details can abound in the realities but not in their recollection.[1]

It is this Borgesian note of disbelief and horror (the details *contaminate with falsity*) that I would like to bring back into our critical discourses about the endless stream of personal anecdote and exiguous but plentiful descriptive detail in contemporary poetry. There is nothing necessarily valuable about the innumerable facts that surround us. If we cannot, in imagination, recollect them, see them as if from afar, then the nearness to trivia that is the inescapable condition of all our lives will contaminate and falsify the very fabric of our thought.

There is another smugness dangerous to poets, which comes not from too little expertise but from too much. It makes the writer too easily infatuated with the measures (in both senses) to which wit resorts. It is an attitude that may too readily turn to epigram and invective, to scowl and barb. This problem, which appears to be related to tone and style, is also related more deeply to the growing vitiation of myths and their implications for belief. In the case of the clever and interesting Derek Mahon from Northern Ireland, we are reminded how little the man of the spirit can depend on traditions. We still live in a society in which, as W. H. Auden remarked three decades ago, "men are no longer supported by tradition without being aware of it." The modern man who wants to bring order into his life is, Auden continued, "forced to do deliberately for himself what in previous ages had been done for him by family, custom, church, and state, namely the choice of the principles and presuppositions in terms of which he can make sense of his experience."

Many contemporary poets solve the problem by turning their backs on the social determinants of tradition and embracing inwardness, which is also to say, wordlessness. Thus they have no direct influence over their own style in the usual sense of maintaining the right to select *les mots justes*: Whatever words fall into place in a consciousness absorbed in the flux of time are, by the nature of the enterprise, the right ones. By contrast, Derek Mahon solves the problem of traditionless modernity by self-consciously applying himself to the unnatural metres, rhymes, stanzas, diction, and tropes of this modified Marvellian tradition, which runs through the eighteenth-century satirists Rochester and Swift to the middle and later work of Yeats. Occasionally, Derek Mahon also obtains the genial clarity of Auden himself in his urban poems:

> Cashel and Angkor Wat
> Are not more ghostly than
> London now, its squares
> Bone-pale in the moonlight;
> Its quiet thoroughfares
> A map of desolation.
> . . . . . . . . . . . . . . . .
>
> A train trembles deep
> In the earth; vagrants sleep
> Beside the revolving doors
> Of vast department stores
> Past whose alarm systems
> The moonlight blandly streams.
>
> ("One of These Nights")

But in general Mahon's satiric work is rough and liable to moments of self-pity in the guise of lyrical concession, while a long poem in accentual triplets about culture in exile, "Ovid in Tomis," flattens out into abstraction-weakened prose.

So Mahon's "solution" begins to seem more problem itself than breakthrough. In fact, this volume is two-thirds exercise, set piece, and warm-up. But the remaining third of *The Hunt by Night* is comprised of poems of such lucidity and modest originality that one can pardon the derivative verse, which may have been the obligatory fodder. Like the solutions of Yeats and Auden but with different temper and give, Mahon's solution is to tunnel back within the dead traditional line until he finds the place where his own voice begins to be audible. Here is Mahon in the town of Portrush on the cold, brutal, rocky northern Irish coast:

> Yet there are mornings when,
> Even in midwinter, sunlight
> Flares, and a rare stillness
> Lies upon roof and garden,
> Each object eldritch-bright,
> The sea scarred but at peace.
> . . . . . . . . . . . . . . . . . . . . . .
>
> . . . the shops open at nine
> As they have always done,
> The wrapped-up bourgeoisie
> Hardened by wind and sea.
> The newspapers are late
> But the milk shines in its crate.
> Elsewhere the olive grove,
> Le déjeuner sur l'herbe,
> Poppies and parasols,
> Blue skies and mythic love.
> Here only the stricken souls
> No spring can unperturb.

The rhythms here are sometimes barely civil to the iambic trimeter model; but the weaving back and forth from the metrical model to his own eccentric rhythm (as in the first stanza above) is Mahon's way to avoid the doggerel that keeps poems like Auden's "Fleet Visit" in the realm of light verse. Unlike Auden in another respect, Mahon never entirely loses sight of the concrete world or describes it categorically, as Auden is apt to do even from the very different impulses that lead to "The Fall of Rome," "Nones," and "In Praise of Limestone." Mahon retrieves the details from merely representative status, both in the particular (milk and newspapers) and in the general, as in the marvelous line, "Each object eldritch-bright."

At the other end of the scale of formal particularity from Auden, Mahon's Scylla, is his Charybdis Philip Larkin, who has made such a success out of the poem that lists. "Show Saturday" from the recently reissued *High Windows* (Farrar, Straus & Giroux) is the furthest Larkin has gone in that direction, with a Stevensian resolution somewhat less satisfying than the endings of "Church Going" and "The Whitsun Weddings" because the scavenging for flotsam is so unrelenting. Indebted to Larkin's corrosive sympathy for the junkyard, where all beloved and even sacred objects are cast in time, Mahon's poem "Garage in Co. Cork" erects a myth of surprising power upon the Larkin descriptive mode:

> Surely you paused at this roadside oasis
> In your nomadic youth, and saw the mound
> Of never-used cement
> Building materials, fruit boxes, scrap iron,
> Dust-laden shrubs and coils of rusty wire,
> A cabbage-white fluttering in the sodden
> Silence of an untended kitchen garden.
>
> Nirvana! But the cracked panes reveal a dark
> Interior echoing with the cries of children.
> Here in this quiet corner of Co. Cork
> A family ate, slept, and watched the rain
> Dance clean and cobalt the exhausted grit
> So that the mind shrank from the glare of it.
> . . . . . . . . . . . . . . . . . . . . . . . . . . . . . . . . . . .
> A god who spent the night here once rewarded
> Natural courtesy with eternal life—
> Changing to petrol pumps, that they be spared
> For ever there, an old man and his wife.
> . . . . . . . . . . . . . . . . . . . . . . . . . . . . . . .
> We might be anywhere . . .
> But we are in one place and one place only,
> One of the milestones of earth-residence
> Unique in each particular, the thinly
> Peopled hinterland serenely tense—
> Not in the hope of a resplendent future
> But with a sure sense of its intrinsic nature.

Note how precarious is Mahon's adaptation to the voice that lists, the communal secular "we," with its reduced, agnostic vantage and the feeling of exclusion that comes to the latest born. Thus one also notes how feeling emerges from the compulsive agnosticism, first by the subtle but lavish play of vowel and consonant over the almost corporeal materials of fence, machine, and garden, then by means of the splendid fiat through which "cobalt" becomes a verb, and then by the grandiloquent pleasantry of the finale, "unique in each particular."

Yet the climax toward which the poem arches and from which these final chords drop down is quite an original move—no less self-conscious in its way than Mahon's use of others' metres and stanzas to the point where they become his own. The allusion to Baucis and Philemon, metamorphosed not into oak and linden but into gasoline pumps, is necessarily a comic travesty, but so is the world of products, brand names, and commercial progress. Mahon is quick throughout the poem to turn from the functionally tawdry to the transiently sacramental, while skirting the dangers of diatribe on the one hand, and on the other, bathos; this, surely, is a genuine accomplishment.

Even subtler performances are the title poem, "The Hunt by Night," on the painting by Uccello (1465), and the companion poem on a very different kind of painting, Edvard Munch's *Girls on a Bridge* (1900). Each shows how a good poet can imaginatively and deferentially engage the inspiration behind another cultural artifact. "Girls on a Bridge" is a much more literal "reading" of a painting than the Uccello; it explores the work in terms of plot: What the three girls can hear from the water; the virginal linen in lamplit bedrooms awaiting them when they go in; what the girls on the bridge might be chattering about among themselves. To this familiar kind of "reading-into" method, however, Mahon adds what at first seems an indirect, but is finally a far more shocking device. He reads into the painting a knowledge of the complete Munch *oeuvre*, from the glancing suggestions of the lesser-known paintings (*Puberty; The Voice*) to the central suggestion of the most famous of Munch's paintings, which, although executed seven years earlier, is conceived as still to come:

> The dusty road that slopes
> Past is perhaps the main road south,
> A symbol of world-wandering youth,
> Of adolescent hopes
> And privileges;
>
> But stops to find
> The girls content to gaze
> At the unplumbed, reflective lake
> . . . . . . . . . . . . . . . . . .
> But wait—if not today
> A day will dawn
>
> When the bad dreams
> You hardly know will scatter
> The punctual increment of your lives.
> The road resumes, and where it curves,
> A mile from where you chatter,
> Somebody screams . . .

Munch's *The Scream* (1893) shows a skull-like face with gaping mouth and horrified sunken eyes apparently rushing along a bridge above a fjord whose sweeping contours repeat the indrawn hollows of the screamer's face. Down the bridge from him, or her, are two utterly upright and well-behaved figures, who might be the future for at least two of Mahon's girls on the bridge; he implies that the third girl may be the one who is screaming.

"The Hunt by Night" is a meditation on the delicacy of Uccello and of the traditions of his period from a vantage ground as it were strewn with imaginary carcasses and rank with bestiality, which belonged to men before they had imposed order on themselves. It is a poem with powerful political overtones, which yet does not try to expose this particular enrichment of its significance straightaway. The "ancient fears" of men in the wild have, by Uccello's time, been tamed to play, though they are still "rampant to" the sound of the hunting horn, "At once peremptory and forlorn." We are reminded of the contrast between what is before us, namely a mild and pungent night peopled with lithe, long-limbed creatures, and, on the other hand, the savagery of appetite. What remind us of blood instinct are the hints about the transitory artifice of this moment, its delicacy, highlighted by Mahon's always decorous compromises here between enjambment and end-line pause:

> The mild herbaceous air
> Is lemon-blue,
>
> The glade aglow
> With pleasant mysteries,
> Diuretic depots, pungent prey;
> And midnight hints at break of day
> Where, among sombre trees,
> The slim dogs go
>
> With wild suspense
> Leaping to left and right,
> Their cries receding to a point
> Masked by obscurities of paint—
> As if our hunt by night,
> So very tense,
>
> So long pursued,
> In what dark cave begun
> And not yet done, were not the great
> Adventure we suppose but some elaborate
> Spectacle put on for fun
> And not for food.

The most courtly and mannered of Derek Mahon's poems, "The Hunt by Night" is also the most natural vehicle in the volume for his multiple gift of cultivation, verbal sophistication, rhetorical daring, high descriptive subtlety and accuracy, and public conscience.

**NOTE**

1. "The Immortal," trans. James E. Irby, in *Labyrinths,* by Jorge Luis Borges (New York: New Directions, 1964), pp. 116–17.

# From "Among the Shades"

David Ferry dwells almost exclusively in the realm of balance and stasis, control and form. An intent inward gazing limits the subjects and reach of his volume of interconnected pieces, *Strangers, A Book of Poems*, creating a natural interplay between the contemplative cast of mind and the literal contemplation of a literal world. These laconic attitudes and a thoroughgoing narrowness of survey saturate his work, completely filling every open area and neutral scene with an atmosphere of foreboding coextensive with life itself. The book is punctuated and defined by deaths, fadings of force, ghosts, and shadows, and even begins with the metaphor of a funerary Etruscan pair disposed among their burial objects just as a modern couple, the speaker and his wife, sit at ease in their livingroom where "Nothing [is] yet utterly lost."

One is not always sure how to read Ferry; the presentation of the visible and the visualizable is always so quick and quiet and solid that the reader may hesitate for some time before realizing that the mood of this poem is lethal, the couple unironically damned, and that they take their nonexistent pleasures with a blind delight.

> *A Tomb at Tarquinia*
> The two of us, on the livingroom couch,
> An Etruscan couple,
> Blindeyed to the new light let suddenly in;

Review of David Ferry, *Strangers, A Book of Poems* (Chicago: University of Chicago Press, 1983); Richard Howard, *Lining Up* (New York: Atheneum, 1984).

Sitting among the things that belong to us,
The style of living familiar, and easy,
Nothing yet utterly lost.

Leapers and dolphins adorn the painted walls;
The sun is rising,
Or setting, over a blue Tyrrhenian Sea;
In the pictured cup the wine brims and glistens;
An unknown flower burns with odorless incense
The still air of the place.

Although this poem could be ingenuously read as a celebration of the timelessly beautiful, it seems to me that the air of the place is thoroughly exhausted. Every certainty of a primary value, like the blueness of the sea, is countered by an ambiguity, such as whether the sun is rising or setting; the movements of living things are countered by being *pictured*, *painted*, and the nouns elsewhere fraught with negatives, *unknown*, *odorless*, even *still*. In my reading of the poem the sun, blue sea, brimming wine, and ancient flower are the sad decorations of a *tomb*, heartbreaking reminders of the life that has fled.

Although he remains quiet in declarative contour throughout "A Tomb at Tarquinia," the poet uncannily "voices" the punctuation after "familiar," and after "and easy," as if to suggest that the one (ease) is not always the logical corollary of the other (familiarity). In the second stanza too he "voices" the commas after "rising," and "setting," dramatizing the timelessness and unreality of this world while invoking a consciousness that is wont to distinguish rising from setting, and that would want to know which was which. And the poet intrudes time into timelessness again by throwing the weight of the next two sentences, whose subjects are *wine* and *flower*, upon the verbs in the present tense, *brims*, *glistens*, and *burns*. The last, *burns*, begins as a parallel to the earlier two, hence a qualified and qualified intransitive verb, but we find in the last line that *burns* has taken a direct object, *the flower . . . burns . . . the air*, and further that the phrase *with odorless incense*, which is at first a qualifying one (how does the flower seem to burn? with a kind of odorless incense), must be retroactively understood as an instrumental phrase (what could the flower accomplish any kind of burning *with*? why, with its [resemblance to] incense; this is how it burns the air).

These chronic revisions are at once slight and sophisticated; the change in function of *burns*, for example, comes about through a minor syntactic inversion, an interruption and postponement of the usual sequence of subject/verb/object/modifiers to subject/verb/modifiers/object: "An unknown flower burns with odorless incense / The still air of the place." It is Ferry's ear for the reverberations of slight shifts in order, diction, and rhythm that makes all the words at times, neutral though they are in isolation, begin to strike our ear strangely, each with a talismanic force far exceeding context yet unthinkable apart from it. Consider these phrases from a poem on his great-grandfather, a minister for whom individually the expressions and metaphors would be more natural than the collective phrasing: "the ripening / Fruit, the purity of intention and deed / In the context of blood and error," an utterance whose inherited tones are dampened by a music whose tempo is modern.

A second example of a kind of precision neither mimetic nor metaphoric but somewhere between: "The sound of the plumbing faithfully dying away / Somewhere in the building." The masterstroke is the use of *faithfully* to mean habitually faithful to a certain sequence of acts in which flushing or running the water is followed by the diminishing whine of the water level. It is an observation ideally made by an insomniac or a solitary.

The felicities and the austerities may convince some readers of the interest of these poems by David Ferry, but there is I believe a further dimension that makes the book notable, best illustrated by the suite of poems on old photographs. Ferry is acute on the photographic phenomenon, which in its infancy tended to produce very bad technical representations of people with very great souls—recall the luminous eyes and hard white teeth, the brown small leathery look of the skin and the set mouth of people in the old discolored prints. The poet attends to these as well as to a phenomenon at least as remarkable as the blazing stiffness of the people, namely the deadness of the surfaces—the familiar shut, rejected, foreshortened appearance in the texture of the furniture, cloth, and general gear.

In one of the poems on Eakins's photographic studies, Ferry versifies as follows some data on the process from the *World Book Encyclopedia*: " 'The darkest objects / Reflect almost no light, or none at all, / Causing no changes in the salts in the emulsion.' " Although dark objects absorb into themselves more light and heat than do pale ones, this heaviness of effect in the physical world is contradicted by the optical logic of the photograph. This contradiction in turn is perceived by the poet as yet another manifestation of the gnostic power of images. Dark objects, which photograph by refraining from stirring the salts in the emulsion, are like those catalysts and limiting states—"negatives"—without which "positives" are impossible to make. Like what the alchemists called *l'oeuvre au noir*, the point at the beginning of the great process where the bonds of matter begin to loosen, the river of resemblances bears forward from the past the forms of magical possibility. In Ferry's work, however, the past is a time so far removed from the moment as to be locked away from us, while we in the present time are constrained to witness the intent, joyless onrushing of a now disembodied and objectless primal energy that no longer seeks an object or occasion to transform.

One site of such terrible knowledge, the knowledge that there is meaning in and around a landscape that is closed to us—that indeed meaning is no longer being made with us in mind—occurs in the poem about the Anasazi, the prehistoric Southwest American Indian tribes whose home ground was connected to underground rivers.

> The Anasazi drink from underground rivers.
> The petroglyph cries out in the silence of the rock
> The tourist looks at. The past is beautiful.
> How few the implements and how carefully made
> The dwelling place, against the wind and heat.
> Looking at a photograph, as at a petroglyph,
> How little there is to go on. "The darkest objects

> Reflect almost no light, or none at all,
> Causing no changes in the salts in the emulsion."
>
> ("Photographs from a Book," V)

How little there is to go on. The experience is all evidence, and no significance, thing without thew, fact failing in meaning. He continues:

> In the brilliant light and heart-stifling heat,
> The scratching on the surface of the rock,
> Utterings, scriptions, bafflings of the spirit,
> The bewildered eye reads nonsense in the dazzle;
> In the black depth of the rock the river says nothing,
> Reflectionless, swift, intent, purposeless, flowing.
>
> ("Photographs from a Book," V)

I think one might be willing to approve many poems more harshly stilted than any David Ferry has included here in order to read lines of such fine severity, in which the small tremors of psychology have been quite, quite lost.

Richard Howard's is a more aggressive relation to psychology. The small tremors become not only curious but crucial. His gestures are crabwise and hovering, deferential toward the banal, secretly ready to pardon it to penetrate its faux pas, but above all *interested* in banality, lightness, manners, because he suspects he may not yet have succeeded in taking from them what he may need to know. *Why* he thinks he needs to know more than what the clichéd, stereotypical, and bathetic proclaim by their prepared surfaces is not immediately clear. But the answer may be related to the poet's attraction to the Victorians and the French of the fin de siècle during a period when mannerism was pervasive without being democratic. It is the same impulse that attracts this writer to the impersonation of historical voices, not as a release from his own, rather as the working out of a curse, as if he were condemned to rehearse the small talk of the great or the even smaller talk of the near-great and self-important and half-forgotten like Loti and Louÿs and Garnier, until the use of masks becomes an exercise in psychological cancellation, high camp, and imperious private joke.

The complicated tenor of this attitude is best illustrated in the poet's chronic use of the pun. Repetition, reflection, and reversal comprise his essential medium. The paintings of Corot were "inevitably silver, ineffably silly landscapes"; inasmuch as Baudelaire addressed maggots, "vermin, hence verse!"; for the composer Meyerbeer, "Poise was always . . . pose"; and in another example of paranomasia somewhat closer to simple alliteration than the first three, Verdi is said to have a paradoxically "furtive inflexibility of style." Both varieties of paranomasia cooperate in many finely tuned poems, for example the address to Nadar's photograph of the painter Millet, whom Howard construes as a bad artist whose weakness, made patent in the photo, protects him from our rage: "Contempt / is reckless, for what we might have connived / to attack as a fortress / we are conned into admiring as a ruin." With a little practice one becomes sensitive to the light music of the alliteration here.

In another of the poems based on Nadar, Verdi's great operas evoke, "luminous, voluminous, / voices wrapped in the gift each sex possesses / of not listening to the other." The flurry of adnomination (varying a "root" term with prefixes and suffixes, as "luminous," by a kind of home etymology, is turned into "voluminous")—this flurry of punning settles into a joke out of a farce, the truism that nevertheless reflects what is for many the most extraordinary pleasure of the opera, the blending, emerging, then disappearance of vocal pattern in trios and duets, when the lead voices employ the gift of not listening to each other.

Throughout *Lining Up* the author is helplessly indulgent toward catchphrase and bon mot, with a taste for allusive monstrosity and malapropism on an almost academic scale. One poem, "On Hearing Your Lover Is Going to the Baths Tonight," whose title suggests the long post-Imperial hiatus, is spoken by a fiercely fretful lover driven to depend on a wit that is also titillating. But the oral-sex innuendo makes merely exigent the catchphrase from Heraclitus: "Your fantasy of his / body doing what it does / with yours, only doing so / with others . . . is *that* the difficulty? Then / put yourself at ease: two mouths / have never drunk twice from the same chimera." Howlers are lavish and frequent.

Richard Howard travesties Shakespeare, Keats, James, Proust, Auden in a fashion automatic and at moments embarrassing. He mangles Rilke in concluding the pun-poisoned address to Baudelaire entitled "Carrion (continued)": "Watching that carrion consumed, I knew: / what devours us, how paltry it is; but what / we are devoured by—ah, Charles, how great!" And then he travesties Baudelaire in reaching after the spectral presence of Pierre Louÿs: "You haunt / my frequentations of your great / contemporaries like a thirsty ghost . . . / I read you, *mon semblable, mon Pierre!*" With respect to this same Pierre, more muted echoes (from Dante!) jostle the blandly broken aside, "In his will was no / peace."

To what end, one might ask, has Richard Howard indulged all his wordplay? The question may lead nowhere. Perhaps it is wiser, as Howard himself suggested some years ago in his fine essay on Emily Dickinson (*Prose*, VI, 1973), to address our irritation with method and mode not as problem but as part of the answer; and instead of viewing his oddities as flaws, to see them as the author's solutions, however partial or provisional, to the real problems he has had to confront as a poet. If a heavy imbrication of puns is Howard's solution, what could have been the problem? Nerves? shyness? hero worship or a spirit of willing self-enslavement to tradition or to mentors who embodied that tradition? On a more confidential scale than the anxiety of influence, was it the anxiety of the young toward the powerful and robust, the anxiety of the adolescent who would gladly join the club?

For Mr. Howard, this "club," as we discover in a superb poem with a surprising subject, Ford Madox Ford, turns out just as surprisingly to be—the "Modern," which the poet confesses "it has been my study / to continue, if headway can be something / besides continual parricide." The starting place for this sympathy between Howard and Ford is not modernity in the abstract, however, but Proust, whom both have felt almost obsessionally lured to translate (although Ford did not and Howard hasn't). Once that link is established, the similarities rapidly mount between these unlikely soul mates. Ford "survived originality" (not his own; that of his friends, like Conrad), whereas Richard Howard himself . . .

> whereas I . . .
> I go round on the back of that other life
>     my reading relinquishes
> like the little Egyptian heron that lives
> on the backs of cows. The shoe fits perfectly.
>     *There is no getting beyond*
> *without first getting as far*, you remind me.

("Homage")

The little Egyptian heron is harmless enough, an unusually modest emblem when we recall how blithely this poet traffics in more ambitious currency (history, time, mortality, reputation), and so perhaps not the most reliable one. But consider. To the large, mangy, approximate body of "life" relinquished by reading the masters the poet-heron daintily acts the valet, grooming the transportation, trim and alert on its perch above the herd. The service is neither tragic nor demeaning. To be derivative is thus to be elevated, borne aloft as one travels into the future.

The jewel in the crown of the present book, "Move Still, Still So," justifies the metaphors of "Homage" with a set of historical materials empathically ignited by a uniquely personal energy. The author is also engaged here in a bizarrely Freudian game. He has written an erotic poem about the origins of an aberration in a young girl owing to the delayed mesmerizing of a nympholept. In this double text the pair do not speak; the man is recalled by the woman, now married, and haunted, as she discusses her current marital problems with a psychiatrist: "Before it happens / I don't move, almost not breathing at all, / and I think it's *that*, / the lack of response / he gets discouraged by." In order to spur herself to orgasm, she must reproduce a state into which she had been hypnotically placed, probably without arousal at the time, when the man who wanted to take her photograph thirty years earlier had attempted to make her sit still: "Now try it a few / minutes like that, child. / Lovely, lovely—one hardly sees why / *this* little princess / should ever need be / covered up by dreadful crinolines." And then as she is swathed in the figurative language of faery to distract her from her deshabille, the photographer had told her about Princess Perdita, whom Florizel saw dancing by herself and commanded, "When you speak, sweet, / I'd have you do it ever. . . . When you do dance, I wish you / a wave of the sea, that you might ever do / nothing but that, move still, still so, / and own no other function" (*The Winter's Tale*, IV.iv). And then the photographer, who is of course Charles Dodgson (Lewis Carroll) explains:

> that's what photographs
> can do, make you a wave of the sea
> that you might ever
> do nothing but that
> . . . . . . . . . . . . . . . . .
> There we are, ready. Now Gladys, dear,
> I want you to lie
> still, perfectly still.
> I'll help you do it, but the impulse
> must be your own. Three
> minutes of perfect
> stillness will do for both you and me.
>
> ("Move Still, Still So")

One could speculate that all erotic love is a profound distortion of an ordinary state of being, so that even fixation on a certain fetish or controversial posture or trick is finally less remarkable than the primal fact itself, that we are invaded by the requirement of another's specific presence. In this extraordinary poem, as in all of Richard Howard's most daring excursions, the aberrant becomes the measure of the universal by being shown from a vantage far back of the point where it becomes strange and well before it hardens into pun and parody. Here, it is simply understood.

# Weeds in Tar

Adrienne Rich may have prefigured what was to happen in her own body of poetry when she wrote of the death of Hadrian, the emperor whose name shadows her own:

> . . . once mere consciousness had turned its back,
> The frescoes of his appetite would crumble,
> The fountains of his longing yawn and crack.
>
> And all his genius would become a riddle,
> His perfect colonnades at last attain
> The incompleteness of a natural thing;
> His impulse turn to mystery again.
>
> ("Villa Adriana," 1955)

The smoothly handled but mannered prosody of the verses in this poem by Rich rather masks the coming decay of order and rule, which she threatens will be as absolute as the turn to impulse, irregularity, incompleteness and mystery. At the same time, the stanzaic symmetries throw a cold dew over the marble excavations and the imperial will these once represented. Almost from the beginning of her career, Adrienne Rich mistrusted the products of tradition, even as she perforce used only traditional forms to express this suspicion, as in "Ideal Landscape," the first poem in the current selected volume, in which the inviting formal nook, glimpsed for a moment in a foreign city, cannot then be rediscovered in reality or on any map. Instead, "the human rose to haunt us

---

Review of Adrienne Rich, *The Fact of a Doorframe: Poems Selected and New 1950–1984* (New York: W.W. Norton, 1984).

everywhere." Never again would the traveler be able to find "those fountains tossed in that same light, / Those gilded trees, those statues green and white."

Twenty years later, in place of these squares and gildings and dusky hints of desuetude, the works of another landscape architect give life to place by resisting the picturesque. This new architect, Rich's alter ego, finds her ink turning to irrigating rain, her park stretching outside its rigid enclosures ("purdah, the salon, the sweatshop loft, / the ingenuity of the cloister") to embrace a mysterious horizon ringed with volcanoes, as her imagination throbs with unborn, inchoate life. The strong free verse is tightly composed:

> I am I,
> this India ink my rain
> which can irrigate gardens, terraces
> dissolve or project horizons
> flowing like lava from the volcano of the inkpot
> at the stirring of my mind.
> ("The Fourth Month of the Landscape Architect," 1973)

The tiny syntactic inversion almost swallowed by the enjambment (this ink can "terraces / dissolve") may be the only sign in the collection from which it comes (the poem is not included in the current volume) that the poet ever consorted with the rhetoric and tropes of Milton. For the most part, Rich has by this time (the publication of *Poems New and Selected, 1950–1974*) converted entirely to free verses, first-person declarations, and (in place of redundancy of stress and measure) the redundancies of evidence, data, and catalogue in frequent parataxis (see, above, the series *purdah, salon, loft, cloister*).

Rich has also given up her early European nostalgias, and giving up Europe for Rich means giving up patriarchy: Milton and Hadrian, architecture and empire are, predictably, equivalent with male domination. America, resistance, and wilderness, on the other hand—kin, quiltwork, and crafts—are the sites of true work and grace. So instead of conquered terrain and aesthetic artifact, Rich has settled upon images of evanescent being, practical daydream, and fiery persistence. As Eleanor Wilner observes in her fine essay on *Poems New and Selected, 1950–1974* (in *APR*, March/April 1975), the volcano image smouldering in this book is a kind of "female apocalypse" in a landscape that is unashamedly totemic. Other poems from the same time as "The Fourth Month of the Landscape Architect" support Wilner's striking claim. "Blood-Sister" ends in a desert "where survival / takes naked and fiery forms" (1974). "The Wave" (1973) is a visible as well as invisible force, the "blankness underlying" everything and the "caldron of all life." And the poem that closes that volume presents female counterparts inhabiting a desert realm where the ridges of a gorge are sexual ("the rose and violet vulva of the earth"). These foldings briefly disclose, as darkness fills them, "a single sparkle / of red, a human fire" ("From an Old House in America," #12, 1974). The sly sparkle at the erotic center would seem to be the provenance of the woman alone, to be reached with intuitive intelligence rather than formal, phallic engineering. Although the decorum of the diction is briefly broken by the reference to genitalia, the eight couplets of this allegorical vignette actively contain and consciously monitor the shock. The calm rising of the evening star reasserts the poet's control as well: ". . . a human fire / and near and yet above[,] the western planet / calmly biding her time."

In the book that comes after *Poems New and Selected, 1950–1974*, Rich adds to her portfolio of volcanic images a love poem (the eleventh of the "Twenty-One Love Poems" composed between 1974 and 1976) in which the term "sacred mountain" denotes the body of homoerotic (Lesbian) passion "smoking within like the sybil stooped over his [sic] tripod." As the lovers climb the peaked crater, the speaker feels the beloved's "arteries glowing in my clasp," and both women observe the radiant emblem of their bond, "the small, jewel-like flower / unfamiliar to us . . . that clings to the slowly altering rock" (*The Dream of a Common Language*, 1978). At once, one recognizes the increased mastery of language: "[A]ltering" applied to rock is one of the clues. Furthermore, this poetic translation of Eros into landscape and of stages of desire into hot crater and cool, unfamiliar petal, performed under the sign of sibylline divination, compels our awe and belief as only strong management of allegory can do.

To continue briefly with the theme of volcanic power, a theme I take as one signal of Rich's discovery of her mature material, we might look at three verse paragraphs from another poem that treats spiritual fire as evanescent. The poem is fueled, moreover, by the rejection of European texts. The descriptive effects are rendered in a fluid yet fiery non-metrical verse.

> Anarchy of August: as if already
> autumnal gases glowed in darkness underground
> the meadows roughen, grow guttural
> with goldenrod, milkweed's late-summer lilac,
> cat-tails, the wild lily brazening,
> dooryards overflowing in late, rough-headed
> bloom: bushes of orange daisies, purple mallow,
> the thistle blazing in her clump of knives,
> and the great SUNFLOWER turns
>
> Haze wiping out the hills. Mornings like milk,
> the mind wading
> . . . . . . . . . . . . .
> the prism hanging in the windowframe
> is blank
> A stillness building all day long to thunder
> as the weedpod swells and thickens
> No one can call this calm
>
>             Jane Addams, marking time
>             in Europe: *During most*
>             *of that time I was absolutely at sea*
>             *so far as any moral purpose was*
>                 *concerned*
>             *clinging only to the desire to live*
>             *in a really living world*
>             *refusing to be content*
>             *with a shadowy intellectual*
>             *or aesthetic reflection*
>             ("Culture and Anarchy," 1978)

The active volcano of feminine aesthetic (and moral) power is glowing and blazing in ground, sky, and plant, rather than exploding in destructive anger; although the tenor of the moment is one of pause and postponement before a torrent breaks, the storm itself does not arrive to sweep all struggling women into dramatic victory. Victory is gradual and steady, taking up the rhythms of the cooling earth.

> Early dark: still raining; the electricity
> out. On the littered table
> a transparent globe half-filled
> with liquid light, the soaked wick quietly
> drinking, turning to flame
> that faintly stains the slim glass chimney:
> ancient, fragile contrivance

The kerosene globe lamp is a powerful natural symbol of the steady mental heat the poet wishes to suggest—one of the strangest and loveliest of Rich's testaments to the tenacity of a strictly feminine intellectual temper.

A final codicil to this sketch of the metaphors of energy, volcanic and eventual: Rich has written a very fine essay on Emily Dickinson called "'Vesuvius at Home.'" In this ground-breaking essay, she makes for the Amherst poet (who devised, says Rich, "a life deliberately organized on her terms") a claim that illuminates her own poetic aims: "More than any other poet, Emily Dickinson seemed to tell me that the intense inner event, the personal and psychological, was inseparable from the universal; that there was a range for psychological poetry beyond mere self-expression" (*Parnassus*, Fall/Winter 1976). Has it not also been Adrienne Rich's aim to find her own way of expressing "intense inner event" in a language that would be as fresh as her feeling? Her career and demeanor suggest that one thing language ought *not* do was simply plod metrically forward. Starting with her third volume, *Snapshots of a Daughter-in-Law* (1963), she realized that metrical verse was not as viable for her as it had been for Dickinson; since then, she has been trying to find both metaphors and patterns of discourse to embody her mistrust of finish.

She has frequently stepped wrong, as many critics have pointed out, but she has not been entirely without success in working her way past accentual-syllabic measures. Her first stage was the loosened blank verse of the reply to the Hadrian poem, "Antinous: The Diaries" (1959), where the passive lover of Hadrian (like the constrained poet who had earlier written about that emperor) revolts against past performance, vomiting up "in part what I've swallowed from glasses, eyes, / motions of hands, opening and closing mouths, / isn't it also dead gobbets of myself . . .?" The next stage of Rich's evolving prosody was the loose accentual line of three and four beats (which Robert Lowell made so attractive), for example in section 9 of her "Snapshots of a Daughter-in-Law" and in many of the poems in *Necessities of Life* (1966) and early in *Leaflets* (1969): "That day I found / the corpse-plants, growing like / shadows on a negative / in the chill of fern and lichen-rust . . . sickness of the rot-smell of leaves / turned silt-black, heavy as tarpaulin" ("The Corpse-Plant," 1963). She returns to this accentual line throughout her oeuvre.

We also see in "The Corpse-Plant" evidence of another trait peculiar to Rich's poetry. Few writers are drawn as she is to metal, mineral, and mildew, the rough and ragged, the cycles of decay—in short, the mottled and unattractive. It is as if she were also declaring her mistrust of elegance by asserting the poetic value of "fern and lichen-rust," "the rot-smell of leaves . . . heavy as tarpaulin"—the patently unsavory. She admires the bog with its hungry pitcher plants; feels drawn deep to a forest interior where the logs rot; is moved to describe strips of tar where surprising weeds flower; likes field flowers like milkweed and mallow, bits and shards like the wasp's nest and pieces of ancient lamp-saucers; admires mineral faces and rock-shelves; and one notes, too, the inevitable exchanges of gases and salts. Even fire is a cauldron of matter into which she looks "as into a mirror, yes, / the serrated log, the yellow-blue / gaseous core / the crimson-flittered grey ash" ("Burning Oneself Out," 1972). Yeats's famous lines, "Whatever flames upon the night / Man's own resinous heart has fed," have not quite the same physical alchemy. Rich is writing from within sensation, not in its archive.

Beginning in the *Leaflets* volume, Rich also begins experimenting with the ghazal couplet, which provided a grid for thematic break and juxtaposition, as well as prompting a rhetoric of pronouncement, while supporting iambic melody.

> I tell you, truth is, at the moment, here
> burning outward through our skins.
> . . . . . . . . . . . . . . . . . . . . . . . . . . . . . .
> The clouds are electric in this university.
> The lovers astride the tractor burn fissures through the hay.
> . . . . . . . . . . . . . . . . . . . . . . . . . . . . . . . . . . . . . . . . . . . . . . . .
> These words are vapor-trails of a plane that has vanished;
> by the time I write them out, they are whispering something
>     else.

> ("Ghazals: Homage to Ghalib," 1968)

The ghazal principle grounds the long, unfocused "Shooting Script" of 1970 with its rash, disconnected metaphors, and thereafter leaves the repertory (though couplet arrangement does not). But the one experimental form whose discovery significantly changed the shape and rhythm of Rich's thought was the poem of open typography that insists on breaths within lines, interpolated material (including prose) from other sources, particularly historical ones, and, again, the even stronger grip of the rhetorical method of juxtaposition with its clear polarity between analogy on the one hand, and contradiction and paradox on the other.

At least two of her contemporaries were moving in this direction at the same time, both very different from Rich: Donald Finkel (in *Answer Back*, 1968, and *The Garbage Wars*, 1970) and Denise Levertov (in *To Stay Alive*, 1971, and *Footprints*, 1972). Of the three, doubtless Rich was still the most reverent toward traditional literary culture, the most careful in establishing the basis of association, so that at the close of a poem like "Planetarium" (*The Will to Change*, 1971), she earns the identification with Caroline Herschel (the astronomer's sister) as well as the exuberant formlessness of the "pulsations" to which both are attuned. In the class of typographic field poems that interpolate historical material, I would also rank highly "Meditations for a Savage Child" from *Diving into the Wreck* (1973), "Phantasia for Elvira Shatayev" from *The Dream of a Common Language* (1978), and the superior pastiche "Culture and Anarchy" from *A Wild Patience Has Taken Me This Far* (1981), from which I quoted above. (This might be the place to observe, with Ellen Moers, that Rich has a puzzling bent toward inappropriate titling; in the case of the poem titles, the inappropriate quality derives from phrases within the text that are lifted to the top, hence we are really observing her tendency toward contorted ad hoc phrasing in the work itself—a tendency that grows more prominent in the 1970s.)

In this light, it is also important to note that Rich's prosodic excursions are bland relative to the enormous rhetorical risks which, brave though they may be, have resulted in so many unrelievedly bad poems. Self-pity and the arousal of ego are not as rare as one might expect from a poet with so strong a sense of mission. But strength of mission does not absolve the arbitrary speech cast up in its wake. Indeed, Rich even claims that the use of bad speech is a necessary stage in the search for a new kind of (political) action. "I want you to listen / when I speak badly," she asserts in "Tear Gas" (1969), preferring to speak "not in poems but in tears / not my best but my worst," thereby riddling her aesthetic resolve with loopholes, padding her art with excuses for being ill-formed and even arrogant in its sentimental self-projections. In a poem where a man has refused to hold an elevator door open for her ("—*For god's sake hold it!* / I croak at him.—*Hysterical,*—he breathes my way"), the rattled speaker returns to her flat to make coffee, listen to a Nina Simone album, open her mail, and think about her lover. But in her mail is a letter from a twenty-seven-year-old prison inmate: "*My genitals have been the object of such a sadistic display / they keep me constantly awake with the pain.*" Rich responds that "my incurable anger, my unmendable wounds / break open further with tears, I am crying helplessly, / and they still control the world, and you are not in my arms" ("Twenty-One Love Poems," IV, 1974–1976).

Misanthropic energy fuels several distortions here, one the exaggeration of all feeling by the major condition of being in love, second the salacious horror produced by quotation, in this context, of the account of the prisoner's abuse by other men. That Adrienne Rich responds to these things strongly is not in question. What is in doubt is whether such feelings warrant communication in this rough, plangent, diaristic form untouched by proportion, moral discipline, the broader context of virtue and action. In other words, I would question the use and perhaps even the rectitude of an art based on the chronic opening of one's sensibilities to anecdotes of victimization. The imagination becomes hardened not by indifference but by gothicism and violence. Yet as Milan Kundera writes, "When the heart speaks, the mind finds it indecent to object. In the realm of kitsch, the dictatorship of the heart reigns supreme."[1]

In her weaker moments, the poet oscillates between two kinds of dictation by the heart. One automatized mode of feeling stems from her anger at fakery and distortion, which further feeds her belief (touched upon earlier) that older formal modes are vitiated.

> . . . we have to pull back from the incantations,
> rhythms we've moved to thoughtlessly,
> and disenthrall ourselves, bestow
> ourselves to silence, or a severer listening, cleansed
> of oratory, formulas, choruses, laments, static
> crowding the wires.
>
> ("Transcendental Etude," 1977)

Odd, how the poem resorts to oratory and the formulas of evidence to argue its negations of oratory and casuist formula. This first nexus of strongly conventionalized response is seconded by the writer's familiar anger at, and helplessness before, the world's victims, whom she would avenge with a fervor whose metaphors (but not whose dry diction and rhythms) echo Sylvia Plath: "When I dream of meeting / the enemy, this is my dream: // white acetylene / ripples from my body / effortlessly released / perfectly trained / on the true enemy // raking his body down to the thread / of existence / burning away his lie

/ leaving him in a new / world; a changed / man" ("The Phenomenology of Anger," 1972).

Her revolutionary impatience, which I would also identify with sentimentality—the conventionalized and automatic—has only reinforced her mistrust of formed, behaved language (rigorous order is the "lie" she will sacrifice herself to burn away. We recall Emily Dickinson's volcano, which she called "The Solemn—Torrid—Symbol— / The lips that never lie—," #601). Adrienne Rich's redoubled mistrust of language in turn has exaggerated her habit of association between self and world in projections of "intense inner event" on a universal scale; in one poem, "blighted elms, sick rivers, massacres" should be, she says, construed as "mere emblems of our own failed freedom"; in another, "everything outside our skins is an image / of this affliction." Metaphor can easily break down into polemical confusion between subject and object.

> A wild patience has taken me this far
>
> as if I had to bring to shore
> a boat with a spasmodic outboard motor
> old sweaters, nets, spray-mottled books
> tossed in the prow
> some kind of sun burning my shoulder blades.
> Splashing the oarlocks. Burning through.
> Your fore-arms can get scalded, licked with pain
> in a sun blotted like unspoken anger
> behind a casual mist.
>
> ("Integrity," 1978)

Whereas rhetorical tropes like epic simile live on in such excerpts, bringing in patently exotic material for comparison, the analogies above also cancel the breadth of learning and wonderment in true epic simile by introducing elements of setting that seem, at best, dully realistic while carrying on the resentments of pathetic fallacy; the sun, one among several items composing the experiential "nature" through which the speaker has had to travel, now folds back on its figural origins "like unspoken anger / behind a casual mist."

In some poems the comparisons become more real and present than the subject terms.

> The tragedy of sex
> lies around us, a woodlot
> the axes are sharpened for.
> The old shelters and huts
> stare through the clearing with a certain resolution
> —the hermit's cabin, the hunter's shack—
> scenes of masturbation
> and dirty jokes.
> A man's world. But finished.
> They themselves have sold it to the machines.
> I walk the unconscious forest,
> a woman dressed in old army fatigues
> that have shrunk to fit her, I am lost
> at moments, I feel dazed
> by the sun pawing between the trees,
> cold in the bog and lichen of the thicket.
> Nothing will save this, I am alone,
> kicking the last rotting logs
> with their strange smell of life, not death,
> wondering what on earth it all might have become.
>
> ("Waking in the Dark," 1971)

What begins in the strictest provisionality (the woodlot of sex) opens into the most detailed verisimilitude (the logging camp with its abandoned outbuildings and their taint of solitary male lust; the speaker's army fatigues—hand-me-downs from a warrior code that can fit her only by shrinking; even the "sun pawing between the trees"), which tend to make the sexual aspect hypothetical and the woodlot quite real. Which is also to weaken the poem's polemical thrust.

But there is another kind of provisionality along with those of form and rhetoric through which Adrienne Rich has opened her poetry to her real subject, the use of disuse, of idling, of turning away from grand gesture and virtuoso theatrics. Although she alerts us to the way Emily Dickinson toys with the "orthodox 'feminine' role" of the creature who is "receptive rather than . . . creative, listener rather than musician," she herself has been attracted to the moment of hiatus and aimlessness as a model for the artist, thereby avoiding both the formalism she early rejected and the demagoguery that occasionally seeps in to fill the blank left by discarded forms. And although Rich's work does not seem to progress from uncertainty to certainty, and hence still falls into platitude and excess, there is no doubt that on poignant occasions the desire to reform and the urge for honest sight and speech cooperate in poetry of great warmth and beauty.

> as if a woman quietly walked away
> from the argument and jargon in a room
> and sitting down in the kitchen, began turning in her lap
> bits of yarn, calico and velvet scraps,
> laying them out absently on the scrubbed boards
> in the lamplight, with small rainbow-colored shells
> sent in cotton-wool from somewhere far away,
> and skeins of milkweed from the nearest meadow—
> original domestic silk, the finest findings—
> and the darkblue petal of the petunia,
> and the dry darkbrown lace of seaweed;
> not forgotten either, the shed silver
> whisker of the cat,
> the spiral of paper-wasp-nest curling
> beside the finch's yellow feather.
> Such a composition has nothing to do with eternity,
> the striving for greatness, brilliance—
> only with the musing of a mind
> one with her body . . .
>
>                   ("Transcendental Etude," 1977)

The passage is based on a concession: The woman's absorption in her 'handiwork' is increasingly deep but as ephemeral as the mental composition of her life that results, the composition in turn as vaporous as the trails of the poem in "Ghazals" that vanish before they can be read, or as glancing as the "mirror lost in a brook" in "Shooting Script," "an eye reflecting a torrent of reflections." The woman's materials and method of achievement come before us as accidental, while her instincts are flawless. Like the weeds in "When We Dead

Awaken" (1971), images of tenacity and blessing conceived by the poet to flourish here and there in tar, the seeds of Adrienne Rich's aesthetic are borne by the wind to fall on dead ground, then perhaps to crop up briefly—and brilliantly—after a little rain. But, scrappy and tenacious as they are, they do not respond to the known techniques of cultivation.

**NOTE**

1. Milan Kundera, *The Unbearable Lightness of Being*, trans. Michael Henry Heim (New York: Harper & Row, 1984), p. 250.

# From "Thick and Thin"

Although I have for several years admired the poetry, at once naïve and graceful, of Gjertrud Schnackenberg, I must take issue with some of the notions that have been aired in its regard. *Publishers Weekly* claims that her second book of poems "is mostly composed of rhyming verse," when less than half the book is comprised of rhyming verse (only thirty-three of the seventy-three pages of text). At the other extreme, her publishers in their jacket copy promulgate the error that the long Chopin poem, "Kremlin of Smoke," is written in "free verse" (when five of the eight sections are in blank verse, the other three in accentual lines of five and six beats—and of course this error was picked up by reviewers), just as they imply that the "light verse" that appears in this second volume is informal or untraditional, unlike the "elegiac and traditional forms of her first," when in fact the light verse is the least satisfying, perhaps, but undeniably the most rigid in respect both to rhythms and rhymes among the new poems (see "Two Tales of Clumsy," "Love Letter," and "Sonata").

These mistakes, born of indifference if not ignorance, complement one another and show how unrewarding it is for any poet to bother writing in traditional forms: The very existence of such a tradition, given the want of audience, is called into doubt. Nevertheless, wherever Schnackenberg's work is de-

---

Review of Gjertrud Schnackenberg, *The Lamplit Answer* (New York: Farrar Straus Giroux, 1985); Amy Clampitt, *What the Light Was Like* (New York: Knopf, 1985); Eleanor Wilner, *Shekhinah* (Chicago: University of Chicago Press, 1984); John Koethe, *The Late Wisconsin Spring* (Princeton, N.J.: Princeton University Press, 1984).

scribed or reviewed, it is cited for its "formalism" (as if we
agreed on what that might mean), and indeed the ability to
rhyme conventionally may seem now quite an achievement—
given the number of novice rhymesters who get bored with
the constraints they adopt and who, like one of the other
poets reviewed here, downshift into half-rhyme or mere allit-
eration. In the same way, the ability to maintain a fairly even,
unpedantic rhythm for a number of lines in sequence may
strike a reading public unaccustomed to any sort of meter as
novel and ingenious.

But Gjertrud Schnackenberg's formalism is striking pre-
cisely because it is not quite natural and easy—because, as it
happens, it *is* artificial and somehow appealingly askew. In
this she differs from more thoroughgoing and sophisticated
formalists writing today, like Turner Cassity, Timothy Steele,
and (when he writes in meter) Charles O. Hartman, not to
mention the Augustans of an older generation like Richard
Wilbur, Howard Nemerov, early James Merrill, Daryl Hine,
the somewhat crustier and more blunt Mona Van Duyn, and
so forth—all of whom tune the forms to their temperamental
purposes: They know how to adjust the degrees of seeming
effort, from effects very baroque to those quite smooth. Nor is
she as brilliantly aggressive in her seizing of form as were
Adrienne Rich and Sylvia Plath in their apprentice volumes.
Rather, Schnackenberg—and I say this with all respect due
her accomplishment—is still very much corralled by and obe-
dient to her use of convention, with an effect often winsome,
sometimes wistful, on rare occasions faintly bored, these being
the responses of any good child trying to learn and to please.

For she is above all a cultivated child. She resembles the
childlike Elizabeth Bishop, but in a more somber key: fresh,
but sedulous; sharply touching and perspicuous, yet tending
to drone and repeat. The negative qualities are almost un-
avoidably triggered by the positive ones—occupational haz-
ards, one might say, of the writer who studies the attitudes of
tireless awe, delight, and tenderness associated with the little
child. These characteristic modes of response are very hard to
render convincing. Elizabeth Bishop manages, in a score of
deliciously precarious poems, to express a child's wonder in

terms almost as endearing (and also, perhaps, as close to cloying) as a child might use herself, while refraining from that final temptation of the adult, explanation. As emblems embodying innocence, Bishop uses techniques of un-finish, leaving behind in her poems occasional clumps of happy, untidy makeshift: repeating herself up to the very doorsill of tiresomeness, or indulging in somewhat too knowing, too insistent non sequitur, or interrupting herself with deprecatory chagrin—all the while training the verse on a vividly illuminated, quasi-magical, yet oddly domestic natural and social world.

Gjertrud Schnackenberg takes many of the same risks. In her poem on Simone Weil, the poet twists the *agon* of the French-Jewish Roman Catholic convert-mystic, who died from a hunger fast in England during World War II, into nursery-poem contortions, trusting that out of the imposed simplicity some true version of Weil's genius as well as her moral complexity might emerge. The poet is virtually sluggish, as if stunned, in her obsessive returns in the poem to the fact of the poor grass clinging to poor soil as metaphor for tenacity of spirit: "I think the grass alone / Can hold within its grasp / What matters to it most, // And still it looks bereft, / And famished as the stones. . . . Only the stones at first / Seemed to have a part in this, / And the little height of the grass. . . . As if the soil itself / Were all that's left on earth, / And all the earth were held / Within its famished grasp" ("The Heavenly Feast"). Inwoven with these images of biblical barrenness in the twenty-nine Hardyesque trimeter quatrains of "The Heavenly Feast" are references to the fast itself—Simone Weil's statements about being unable to eat while her brothers and sisters were starving; she asks her ration to be sent to them for "it is theirs"—and a further metaphoric strand in which the birds of the earth "toil to paraphrase" Weil's message. A finch "tries and tries. . . . It is theirs, she seems to say, / Or that is what I hear. . . . I swear I can hear the words, / Send it to them, they say, / Send it to them, it is theirs." The birds then (as a child might imagine it) bear the sufferer's wasted body up to paradise where God tries to help her eat.

Although I was, at first, put off by the Weil poem, finding it

I suppose more than anything to lack comprehensive insight into the author of *The Need for Roots*, "The Love of God and Affliction," and "The *Iliad* as a Poem of Force," I have begun to like "The Heavenly Feast" for its risk in reducing the mind and mission of Simone Weil to such hard, sweet, and banal terms. The terms provide only a partial portrait of the elusive woman at its core, but also a total expression of one kind of ingenuous and loving response to her virtue: The poem leaves nothing to be desired that it desired to do. A thimble is only as full as a thimble can be.

The poem "Supernatural Love," on the other hand, a far more sophisticated poem, occupies a more ample arena. The rhymed pentameter triplets describe the poet-speaker as a child of four sewing her embroidery (she is doing the word "Beloved" on her sampler—hence precocious culturally as well as manually) as her scholar-father at the dictionary stand in his study looks up etymologies for words his child has uncannily associated. Like the Simone Weil poem, however, "Supernatural Love" posits a childlike mystery that an adult must explore, except that here the hidden core of intuitive knowledge is coextensive with the early self of the poet and writer: "My dangerous, bright needle's point connects / Myself illiterate to this perfect text // I cannot read. My father puzzles why / It is my habit to identify / Carnations as 'Christ's flowers.'" Meanwhile, she imagines in the room "Christ's fragrance" from flowers whose "stems squeak in my scissors, *Child, it's me*." The child has no good reasons for identifying Christ with carnations beyond her belief in this visitation. She connects Christ with her father—overwhelming yet familiar, incarnating himself (the pun the father tries to fathom at the dictionary) in the most fairy-tale-like objects, which the child's sewing instruments cut across and transpierce: Her scissors cut Christ's stems, her needle and stitches catch at both meaning and her own flesh in the word she sews. Meanwhile, the father reads about *Carnatio*, "a pink variety of Clove,"

> "From French for *clou*, meaning a nail."
> He gazes, motionless. "Meaning a nail."
> The incarnation blossoms, flesh and nail,

I twist my threads like stems into a knot
And smooth "Beloved," but my needle caught
Within the threads, *Thy blood so dearly bought,*

The needle strikes my finger to the bone.
I lift my hand, it is myself I've sewn,
The flesh laid bare, the threads of blood my own.

. . . . . . . . . . . . . . . . . . . . . . . . . . . . . . . . . . . .

My father's hand touches the injury

As lightly as he touched the page before,
Where incarnation bloomed from roots that bore
The flowers I called Christ's when I was four.

("Supernatural Love")

Witty in its devotions and as idiosyncratic as Elizabeth Bish-
op's religious poems "Roosters" and "The Weed" (echoing
George Herbert's eerie charm), Schnackenberg's poem is also
about the poet's love for her dead father whose mild, highly
composed temperament rises from the gestures of peering,
bending, and touching the pages of his reference books. Like
the elegy for her father that appears in *Portraits and Elegies*
(1982—along with a second poem, reprinted here, the superb
"Darwin in 1881"), "Supernatural Love" identifies the father
with the lens that helps him fix the object of study in the halo
of his respectful attention. The scholar's bending attitude pro-
duces a result so momentous the poet extracts the phrase for
her new book's title: "My father at the dictionary-stand / Tou-
ches the page to fully understand / The lamplit answer, tilting
in his hand / His slowly scanning magnifying lens." The
"lamplit answer" (of suffering slowly fathomed as beauty)
comes to the father with respect to the "question" of his inscru-
table small daughter; the "lamplit answer" of her yearning
admiration then comes to that daughter (years later) with re-
spect to her diligent and affectionate (and lost) father; and it
comes to both, by extension, in respect to the certainty of
religious awe and family love in the impersonal modern
world. To this end, the poet's wit and simplicity wonderfully
leaven one another.

Before leaving this volume, I will briefly note that some of
Schnackenberg's most original metaphors come from works

whose general framework is dilatory or flawed, the two long fairy-tale poems—the 362-line "Imaginary Prisons" on the inhabitants of Sleeping Beauty's castle, and the eight-section poem on Frederic Chopin as a child and young man, "Kremlin in Smoke." The latter, the more mannered and ornamental, presents a feverish decadence allied to the pampered prodigy's fondness for flowers and sweets: the salon's "cream cakes, the pale-skinned meringues, / And the candied violets." Camellias and calla lilies are Chopin's favorites, redolent of the hothouses of the wealthy and hinting at his own fragility (he suffered from TB). These exotic flora also represent the dreamy, cruel, suffocating femininity of the age; he twirls

> a creamy camellia, ruffled
> As the hem of the Marquise's gown, through which
> The maid's heavy iron slowly drifted
> That she may longer twirl and twirl beneath
> The arbor where lilacs foam along
> The crest of the waltz craze, though the first
> Mottles of corruption edge the petals,
> Like the tarnish on the scissors which
> Decapitated it: Flowers, because
> I too am an outcome withering from my cause.
>
> ("Kremlin in Smoke")

The two motifs (the confectionary and the floral) frequently combine, as when "tea steam hangs / Phantom chrysanthemums on long, evaporating stems / In the air of the winter apartment," or when, before his recital, his hostess the Marchioness's nasty pet monkey demolishes a flower and flings it aside, "And the powder shaken from the lily's horn / Scatters like crumbs of fire across the floor."

This odd tendency of Chopin's (and the poet's) to see the world as essentially edible, is also subtly at work in the magical transfers from inanimate to animate in "Imaginary Prisons," as when we see the furnace-stoker forever halted in mid-act, "Around whose lifted shovel embers sparkle / And hang like bumblebees around a flower." And in the real prison within the metaphoric prison of the enchantment, the court poet's works are vouchsafed by "angelfish streaming their whispered letters . . . To flee along their unseen, drifting ladders," while the king's birdkeeper, unwittingly lending his own distortion to the uncanny lens of the tale, "Is dreaming that the brass keys of the jailer / Chirp in the locks of manacles and fetters, / Soft as the first in all the aviary / To voice a note before the blackness clears."

These metaphors are very engaging, even if the sentiments they portend are occasionally, as I say, somewhat too sweet. But Gjertrud Schnackenberg may not feel much justice in my objections, preferring instead (and I would not blame her) to abide by the famous advice of Cocteau: What others reproach you with is precisely what you should cultivate, for it is the key to your very being.

Amy Clampitt may well have heeded Cocteau's advice, but she has been saddled with a bundle of idiosyncrasies that will not be to everybody's taste. Her work is always overheated. Like Hart Crane, she is moved to a species of bluster and often, in her striving to be profound, produces verse whose language competes with and obscures experience rather than bearing, clarifying, even on occasion acquiescing to experience. "He'd looked into the murk of so much turmoil, / flux and rigor, unbought *pietas* of the suicidal, / such jigsaw-faultline fracturings of seeming / entity"; "O friable repose of the organic!"; "the tabernacled rods' / implosive marrow"; "lucent with a mindlessness as total / as the romp that ends up wet-mittened, / chap-cheeked, fretful beside the kitchen stove"; "the samphire-gatherer's mimic god-deliverer / still bled metonymy"; "promised landfill, with its lethal asphodel / of fumes, blooms the slow dying of the Hackensack"; the glass of the future is "that coruscating cold-frame fernery of breath"; a cemetery's "plywood and acrylic / itching gimcrack Hebrew like a brand name." The plethora of such examples is, to be frank, astonishing and perhaps a trifle sad. So much energy, so little control.

The jagged, lanky, uncouth, obstreperous language almost pleases more before we bother about meaning. This is also to say that, once we become conscious of the text's urgency to speak its message and of its need to address us in—to be taken seriously as—stanzaic and linear and even grammatical form, the variations and jokes and self-conscious explosions of chatter become too self-canceling to follow, and then even coherence of feeling is gone.

Amy Clampitt is not a poet of feeling or of idea but of perception; her work shows us a world rich in natural life on which a shimmer of knowing appreciation glistens. I do not get the sense that she actually *thinks* about the world (although she has mastered an enormous amount of data about it, which, proud and elliptical and pedantic, she strikingly scatters about); rather, she flaunts it before her sensibility, daring herself as she challenges it to assume more outrageous incarnations of excess. It is no wonder that nominal forms (rhymes, stanzas, metrical lines) should be overborne in the process. What is more disturbing is that *all* her prosodies tend to cacophony.

Two of the eight poems that form an homage to John Keats illustrate the disintegration at each formal extreme, from blank verse to rhymed quatrains, each in a rough approximation of iambic pentameter cadence. In the first excerpt, the line lacks the power to contain the fraying of the prosaic notes the poet uses to render Keats's thought process as he designs his fairy narrative "The Eve of St. Agnes" (the ellipses are Clampitt's):

> No progress with the epic since Tom
> died. Isabella Jones urging him to try another
> romance. Why not, she'd said, the legend
> of St. Agnes' Eve? A girl going to bed . . .
>
> He must have whistled at the notion that struck
> him now. And then blushed. Or vice versa. A
> girl going to bed on St. Agnes' Eve—that very
> night, or near it—without supper, so as to
> dream of the man she was to marry. Imagine
> her. Imagine . . . He blushed now at the
> audacity. But the thing had taken hold:
> St. Agnes' Eve. A girl going to bed . . .
> On the twenty-third of January, they walked
> thirteen miles, to a little town called (of
> all things) Bedhampton.
>
> ("Chichester")

Poor Keats. Beyond the travesty of his consciousness, however, there is that of his linguistic and poetic sensibility. To read down the right-hand margin of the excerpt is to diagnose the deafness of the writer to the norm she pretends to play against, namely conversational blank verse, which *must* assert a linear unit in order that the divergences from that mode be rhythmical, conspicuous, and telling; without a norm, there is no pattern to counterpoint, hence with one exception no rhythm. The exception comes when the looping colloquial spurts approach each line boundary above; then a false dramatic hitch is introduced that forces us to exaggerate the emotional distance between "Imagine" and "Imagine / her," until even the most straightforward expressions are fraught with moment. Consider the theatrical gap that is wedged between prepositions and their objects (*at the / audacity*; *of / all things*), between articles and nouns (*the / audacity*; *A / girl*), between verbs or nouns and their complements (*struck / him now*; *that very / night*; *they walked / thirteen miles*), as if to make the theme of each passage more arcane than it would be in prose. Casual compositional practice thus masquerades as provocative wisdom.

Similarly, in the last of the Keats poems, this one in quatrains, we see another set of allied devices designed to disarm objection. Rhetorically, Keats is viewed through the melting rivery lens of Hart Crane (via the latter's poem "Porphyro in Akron"—Porphyro is the suitor in Keats's "The Eve of St. Agnes"); Clampitt also appends scurrying peripheral glances at Wallace Stevens and Osip Mandelstam. The syntax is a staccato of fragments, although not even the freedom to maneuver afforded by the license to list and compress suffices to free the lines to develop their end rhymes: "[A]nd then he tried to imagine Porphyro in Akron":

> (Greek for "high place"): the casement, the arras,
> the fabricated love nest, the actual sleet storm,
> the owl, the limping hare, the frozen grass,
> Keats's own recurring dream of being warm—
> who'd been so often cold he looked with yearning even
> into blacksmiths' fires: "How glorious," he wrote

of them, shivering (with Stevens) to see the stars put on
their glittering belts: of what disaster was that

chill, was that salt wind the imminence? The cold-
a-long-time, lifetime snow man did not know.
Beside the Neva, Osip Mandelstam wrote of the cold,
the December fog-blurs of Leningrad, O to throw

open (he wrote) a window on the Adriatic!

("Voyages")

It is enough to make one forswear literary allusion for good.

Now Clampitt is not being criticized for rhyming, but for
rhyming badly—that is, for having taken up the challenge of
this interesting linguistic means of holding together likeness
in sound and difference in logic, but then doing it in such a
way that the likeness in sound is lost in excess enjambment.
Hence the lines embraced by rhymes have no integrity, thus
no comparability, and hence the stanzas composed of rhyming
lines offer no grid of balanced imbalance as sentence (syntax)
either coincides or fails to coincide with line. This is not even
to mention the fact that the poet blithely chucks the full rhym-
ing when nothing occurs to her, sometimes in favor of termi-
nal alliteration or near rhyme (*wrote /that*), or accentually-off
rhyme (*arras /grass; even /on*), and sometimes in favor of bald
bad rhyme (from "Voyages": *Orizaba /rubber; Ohio /into; cargo /
through*; and, from a poem in rhymed triplets, a technique that
gets more and more shabby: *accidental /kiln /will; very /no /any;
object /not /unshaped; to /clay /lady; a /pottery /tale*).

These latter liberties result from laziness or arrogance or
both; but the former (rhyme accompanied by too rapid en-
jambment or run-on) are symptoms of a deeper disdain and
distrust of the very reasons for rhyming at line ends. Above
all, neither counts as authentic extension or redefinition of
technique. For like much of the visual and botanical profusion
in her poetry, Clampitt's play with forms is designed to im-
press the uninformed or uninterested with how much she
knows (about plants; about such quaint old things as stanzas
and meters) without convincing or enlightening the (moder-
ately) knowledgeable reader.

The tumble of her language and the exorbitance of her syntax may simply be formally unmanageable, although she achieves something more pleasing out of Hart Crane's shadow and in Marianne Moore's, whose faint fussiness and lightning clarity are audible in many lines of "Gooseberry Fool" ("That veiny Chinese / lantern," "thistles' silvery, militantly symmetrical / defense machineries") and in "Cloudberry Summer" ("pale-jeweled morsels of seed and sweetness," "a dapple of such countless, / singly borne, close-to-the- / ground corollas"). Even the shade of Stevens at his most arch and willful may lighten Clampitt's "the razed, / the *triste*, the unaccounted-for." Unfortunately, these strands of likeness are far outnumbered by the eruptions of overheated but not very winning description ("Mulleins hunker to a hirsute / rosette about the taproot") and a bent toward erudite inebriated nonsense, as in "O Abendland, astral / insomniac, prophetic hulk of the / unuttered."

I am as surprised by Amy Clampitt's fame as by Eleanor Wilner's obscurity, since Eleanor Wilner has many of the things for which the other is given credit: "a keen mind combined with rich feeling"; philosophical acuity (Wilner possesses an original way of treating consciousness); alertness to the history of literary culture; and attention to the fate of the earth. And although Wilner, like Clampitt, has a strong discursive bent, Clampitt's savagely mixed eclectic mode clouds discourse, unlike Wilner's unobtrusive middle style, which bends in the direction of euphony in unexpected ways, giving her poems a transparent ease and loveliness generally lacking in the dense ramblings of the other. Here is an illustrative Wilner passage about the way the Homeric sea bears the voices of those sailors of Odysseus who drowned. Note the function of line break, verbatim repetitions, syllabic repetitions (or alliteration), interior rhyme, and end rhyme to tighten the audible warp of the verse:

> Their sound keeps breaking
> on the shore—the voices of the drowned,
> the unrenowned, the living tide
> incessant, whispering: anonymous,

anonymous, anonymous . . . the foam
left on the stones when the waves
withdraw—transparent roe, ghost spawn,
it glitters for a moment and is gone.

("The World Is Not a Meditation")

One should note as well the careful and ingenious turning of the trope or figure of men as waves, "the living tide," whose expiring leaves only a lace of male seed, "ghost spawn," behind.

Here as elsewhere Wilner's metaphoric gift is truly remarkable, its function to elucidate the relations between mind and experience in the most refreshing way. For example, when the poet fails in her attempt to bring to mind the living presence of Emily Brontë, she compares Brontë's inscrutability to "a passage left in Greek / on a page of English." The end of the world in another poem is said to loom "like a shark's fin on the flats of our horizon." In another she cleverly unravels the conceit of nauseating sweetness in the Garden of Eden. Eve, revolted by the unbearable saccharine cheer of the place, pushes her way out of "that Eden / with its little sickly nightingales / the color of rancid butter, its flowers nodding / in continual agreement, its crickets and / its sticky, sticky rivers." An obvious and delightful contribution is made to this metaphor by the echoic trope (*sickly*, *rancid*, *crickets*, and *sticky, sticky*). And in a poem about the caryatids in the Erectheum of Athens, a horse too exaggerated to be anything but that night-mare which, for its role at Troy, exacts constant subtle reparation from the Greek psyche, breaks from the sea, "water streaming from the white cliffs of his teeth, / wrecks clinging to his coat like burrs." The tact, the aptness of the metaphor and its details, calm us with pleasure even as we assent to the subject's violence.

Whereas thematically Amy Clampitt is static or tautological, despite her invocations to intense emotion—her characteristic gesture is the round-mouthed glistening-eyed apostrophe— Wilner is emotionally cool but thematically elastic and even daring as she draws together theory and sensibility. Although each of these poets tends to rely on a syntax of addition and parallel rather than subordination and reservation, Wilner's method of layering the ancient with the modern inevitably produces more electricity. One of her ways of paralleling is to view contemporary occasions in light of primitive stories. The murder of a sex offender in Germany by a barmaid whose daughter he had molested is viewed in light of the Demeter-Dis-Persephone myth ("six bullets, one / for each of the pomegranate seeds / that stained her daughter's mouth / with red"). Further, in this retelling, the rapist (Dis/Pluto) is not merely the lord of the realm of winter but also (in a Blakean transmutation) a type of Urizen, lord of the realm of the frozen reason—a distorted intellectuality associated by Wilner (who is fond of long reductive cross-cultural schemata) with Rome, paternal oppression, Law, legalized abuse of the psychoanalytic defense, nuclear physics, and modern military might. Against these forces, the victim's voice pitifully cries out, at first for the mother alone to hear above "the roar / of the chariot of Dis. He has split / the earth, the atom, the heart / of the world cracks" ("Eleusis"). But soon after this, Justice enters the picture, as do the Furies (whom she banishes for the time being), graybeard Judges, children who attend the rapist's trial "on an outing for their civics class," and the voice of Hera, which can also be heard stirring up Hell. The narrative reads in places like a rock libretto for a topical *Walpurgisnacht*, for Wilner also wishes to turn the question of culpability in the Klaus Grabowski/ Marianne Bachmeier case into a warning about the effect of winter logic upon the fate of the globe:

> Zeus gave her to his brother for his sport.
> The time grows short; the wounds of earth are
> gaping. . . . A deeper law moves scarlet in its veins.
> . . . . . . . . . . . . . . . . . . . . . . . . . . . . . . . . . . . . . .
> As old men rage in all our capitals,
> as the missiles shuttle on their tracks,
> earth shudders and Persephone
> is rising in the fields, and all the flowers—
> as if the dumb, dishonored earth were given tongues—
> cry out, cry out, cry out.
>
> ("Eleusis")

We are taken rather far afield of the original unsavory news item by this faint crescendo of implication whereby failure to rejoin imagination to will and (life) blood to (gray) matter will result in an apocalyptic (nuclear) shuddering of the earth. Yet the poet's whole energy is pointed toward connecting the new atrocity, the up-to-the-minute miscarriage of justice, back to the Great Chain of Resemblance on which inner and outer, single and social, energy and matter have always been either entangled or resolved. And although in the poem "Eleusis" itself the "mysteries" of unified vision may fit only jaggedly above the contemporary action, resulting in an uneven text, the central insight that joins the rape of Persephone to the death of the soul to the fate of the victim-earth in the atomic age is compelling.

The "enormous blue writhing" of the energy of the sea in "The End of the Line" is a further sign of the melancholy that often accompanies imaginative acts in Eleanor Wilner's poems: The mind is faintly sickened by its own functioning and yearns to enter the realm of sensation rather than thoughts. The world of surface sense, identified with the unselfconscious, goal-less circularity of pure joy, thus comes to shed a sacramental aura over common scenery:

> There is quiet now and the sweet lapping
> of waves, no more tormented
> by the thrashing in their heart . . .
> only the ordinary breeze, the gentle tug
> of tides, the amber light of late sun,
> and far out, farther than the eye can track
> or tired mind imagine
> something blue as midnight,
> more powerful than hope,
> swims free of our thin, killing line.
>
> ("The End of the Line")

The enormous blue writhing leaps and sports "for the sake / of play" and not for profit or empire or artifact or outcome. Several other poems return to this idea that the world reflexively expands with relief, and deer return in glaucous light, once Adam goes. "And the sun, as the earth turns by it, /

writes its changing shadows on the land. / Everything speaks of itself" ("The Continuous Is Broken, and Resumes"). The coerced world, which had turned mute at Adam's step, resumes its old effortless eloquence: "Everything speaks of itself: / the fireflies in their code of light— / short flashes, the long dark in between; / the sand, grain by grain, is a pure reiteration." This return to the circularities of instinct, flesh, and sensation purged of thought is, of course, more viable as antidote to atrophied reason than as a program with a satisfying order of its own. It would promote (and has usually led to) union with the very materiality from which the poet recoils.

At once more pointed than the tone-poems-of-the-mind just cited, and less localized than the poem about the Bachmeier revenge-murder, Wilner's poem about women haunted by medieval religious mentality is yet another and curiously satisfying treatment of perennial motifs as they take immediate specific forms. "Without Regret" is spoken by a chorus of holy women who have been immured in a cloister where life and feeling are suspended. The lord of their enclosure is at once ominously absent, and omnipresent, a type of warrior-thane away on Crusade as well as the beast of whom both lords and ladies have reason to be afraid—a savage image of collective religious terror. In this drear hiatus, the women weave baskets, tend the animals in a barn reminiscent of Bethlehem's, and suffer a series of winter hallucinations. Even the dozen lines I quote will not do justice to Wilner's slow accretion of effect:

> The fields lay fallow, swollen with frost,
> expectant winter. Mud clung to the edges
> of our gowns; we had hung back like shadows
> on the walls of trees and watched. In the little circles
> that our tapers threw, murdered men rose red
> in their clanging armor, muttered
> words that bled through the bars
> of iron masks: the lord
> who sold us to the glory fields, lied.
> . . . . . . . . . . . . . . . . . . . . . . . . . . . . .
> The lord has gone with the hunt, and the snow,
> the snow grows thicker. Well he will keep

till spring thaw comes. Head, hand, and heart—
baskets of wicker, baskets of straw.

("Without Regret")

Like less clever versions of Penelope, the nuns fall into a mild delirium of devotional redundancy, afraid to speak what they know about those bloody armored knights whose belief in holy wars betrayed them, yet unable to break the bonds of their own enchantment to the liturgical year. They are one type of feminine response to mystery—a type with few memorials or apologists—whom the poet images as "Trumpets without tongues" preceded by their flickering candles into the long stony dark of a dead time. The poem is a testament to a further gift of Eleanor Wilner beyond those of clarity, euphony, imaginative vigor, and intellectual appeal: the ability to impersonate profoundly foreign and mysterious human emanations.

Whereas John Ashbery gives the impression of using words *while* he thinks—during and alongside thought, as it were, the words' referents more or less tangential to the real procedures of his consciousness—John Koethe seems to move along *by means of* his attempt to refer, taking the denotative values of words and opening them out further. For neither are words irrelevant. But for Ashbery their individual character and their grace in combination (in *his* artful combination) have less to do with the actual problem he may be working out in a given poem. With Koethe, I believe, the verbal gloss is less stunning, the linguistic and rhetorical gift on the whole less protean and lyrical, but his approach to metaphysical meditation less indirect. He is capable of such apt insights into the cultural tradition as the following: "[H]istory is nothing but a way of talking / About a single moment, of pronouncing the present / So that it seems like the outcome of the sequence of [earlier] styles" ("The Narrow Way"). All the same, Koethe's poems as a rule concern a very earthly stage of mental and spiritual activity when the soul is still ravaged by nostalgia for the trivial comforts of the body and of an almost creaturely memory: "A life reverberating with the low / Echo of love, the echo of lost time, / Time that is over. But the small pleasures /

That come to seem like happiness remain" ("The Echo Chamber"). Koethe's speakers resemble souls who have recently died and still have the habit of association with the carnal, which (by virtue of other longstanding habits) they have always reflexively transmuted into yearning:

> This is a sphere of thought and talk and dreams
> I live in, where the summer light falls lightly,
> And the intact memories of home float up and die
> As an imaginary calm settles over the mind
>
> And is unreal.
>
> ("Dark Bedroom")

> The memories come more quickly, and the world at twilight,
> The world I live in now, is the world I dreamed about
> So many years ago, and now I have.
> How far it feels from that infatuation with the childish
> Dream of passing through a vibrant death into my real life!
>
> ("The Substitute for Time")

Koethe is not adept at embodying other sensibilities (I have in mind the unlikely and unlikable "Dorothy Wordsworth," the more derivative Ashbery imitations, the poems in the Stevensian-hieratic mode of "life is reading and respite from reading," and finally the use of dull declarative explosions that recall the somnambulistic style of the 1950's, for example, "far beyond myself I was a boy / And . . . he was all of heaven that I had"). Furthermore, in his own area, the poet is perhaps too fond of the dissolving emotions, yearning, nostalgia, disembodied remorse, nonspecific elegiac sadness, and so on. He admits that sometime around the middle of his life (he is forty), "my voice took on the accents / Of a mind infatuated with the rhetoric of farewell" ("In the Park"). Rather than seek a cure for this infatuation, however, the poet-speaker passively records its gradual transmutation into unwilled calm before the pageant of strong, bland dreams of happiness that he realizes will never come to be. What he elegizes is his faded middle youth, from the time he left home until the present:

Don't you remember how free the future seemed
When it was all imagination? It was a beautiful park
Where the sky was a page of water, and when we looked up,
There were our own faces, shimmering in the clear air.
And I know that this life is the only real form of happiness,
And sometimes in its midst I can hear the dense, stifled sob
Of the unreal one we might have known, and when that ends
And my eyes are filled with tears, time seems to have stopped
And we are alone in the park where it is almost twenty years
    ago
And the future is still an immense, open dream.

("In the Park")

It is remarkable how close the writer comes to the springs of
regressive human sentiment without becoming sentimental—
despite his tendency to settle in an immature but not yet infan-
tile vision. And although his meditative discipline is consider-
ably impaired by his bent to earthward, still his simplicity and
intellectual reserve sustain him in his quest for a new rhetoric
and, indeed, framework of feeling. His conversational *stillness*
is a marvelous and, I find, seductive tool (as is his prosodic tact
in breaking lines unspectacularly yet coherently) for investigat-
ing what all creative work is ultimately concerned with—how
to lift oneself above time yet remain immersed in feeling.
Consider his subdued yet striking speculations on what poetry
can encompass:

I was wondering the other day
How poetry still manages to move people
(Since any illusions about its ability to do so
Should by now have been definitely dispelled),
And my first thought was that it might somehow be due to
That experience of the movement of experience into memory
That is the breath of time, the static motion of the soul
On the border between sight and silence,
Flux and the mind—or in so many words
The feel of dying without the catch of death
To validate it at the end, seductive and mild
As a wind without the temperament to daze, to fill the eyes,
Refreshing but replacing nothing,

> The style of change without the
> Verifying annihilation.
>
> ("The Narrow Way")

The narrow pathways worn by the French metaphysicals (especially St.-John Perse and Valéry), by great prose brooders like Proust and James, by their verse-followers in the modern and contemporary periods, Wallace Stevens and John Ashbery, are trod by John Koethe with a light and mild and appealing intelligence. His new metaphysical economies may help, along with Schnackenberg's charming simplicities and Wilner's great wide-ranging liveliness, to redirect the course of poetry in our unpropitious time.

# Lessons in Feeling: A Moral Essay

Both Chase Twichell and Galway Kinnell are sensualists. But this is not why my review-essay has the term "moral" in the subtitle: I am not chastising them for being poets of the passionate senses. On the contrary, in identifying the corner of experience they have undertaken to colonize, I am attempting to make it possible to grant the hypothesis, then to ask the central question. Granted (1) that one is interested in their poems in the same way that one is interested in Lord Byron, François Truffaut, or Paul Bowles (for in much of this work the combination of foible and ironic *faiblesse*, carried as lightly as possible, is crosshatched by the grimace of boredom, or of obsession, which chronically threatens unfettered sexual appetite). And granted (2), on the other hand, that when such work fails to engage, it does so in its resemblances to the various uninspired erotic diarists who must rehearse (in order, presumably, upon later reading, to reincite) every stimulation. Given these assumptions and provisos, how do they make meaning?—how do they place meaning in world and in word so as to perform a genuine transformation in our understanding?

Of the two writers, Twichell creates an impression of greater hubris in the service of her ideal of tragic sexuality. This is also

---

Review of Chase Twichell, *Perdido* (New York: Farrar Straus & Giroux, 1991); Galway Kinnell, *When One Has Lived a Long Time Alone* (New York: Alfred A. Knopf, 1991); Eavan Boland, *Outside History: Selected Poems 1980–1990* (New York: W. W. Norton, 1990); Pamela Alexander, *Commonwealth of Wings: An Ornithological Biography* (Hanover, N.H.: University Press of New England, 1991).

to say that she more rapidly expends her imaginative and linguistic resources in her haste to arrive at depth of response, providing insufficient pleasure in her attitudes to pleasure. She creates about her personae a great debris of what I experience as an early exhaustion of emphasis and feeling. The title of her first poem ("Why All Good Music Is Sad") diagnoses this propensity. It is as if, by aggressively raising the banner of her haste in pursuing an idea, she could thereby coerce from each quick start an effect all the more winsome for its stubbornness; yet once this random notion of violence-as-music is on the page, the poet must drive an analogy rashly apprehended toward its swoon of illogicality. We are in the moody tropical paradise perfectly named "Perdido"—a name that overlays the cool, monotonous melody orchestrated by Duke Ellington upon an island landscape of self-conscious forsakenness; the speaker is floating prone on the transparent water:

> I saw the long, bright muscle of a fish
> writhing on a spear, spasm and flash,
> a music violent and gleaming . . .
> Before I knew that love
> would end my wilful ignorance of death,
> I didn't think there was much
> left in me that was virgin, but there was.
> That's why all good music is sad.
> It makes the sound of the end before the end.
>                    ("Why All Good Music Is Sad")

Most readers do not need to be told that this is writing that must achieve its effects in the absence of rhetorical subtlety. And most readers will also feel the not inconsiderable seduction of authorial fervency. The blandness of the syntax only belies the extravagance of the assertions, and of their juxtaposition to one another.

When the poet enacts her recurrent "plot," in which a nostalgic ebbing succeeds the high tides of despair and craving, the reprise characteristically takes the form of lyrical landscape description. In these episodes of ebbing, the poet will consciously insert slivers of unanticipated diction (in the sample below, "crumpled," "blond," "hard . . . wildness"), by whose appearance the artist insists we witness her hand bravely, gamely brandishing an approximation of skill in the face (or so the soft, pitying tone suggests) of almost insuperable emotional pressure: "But it's beautiful here / in this house above the valley, / close to the crumpled / paper of the clouds . . . And words weigh down the long, / soft-spoken branches of the evergreens, / weigh the unpruned / branches of abandoned orchards / down into the blond grass / where the pears, / grown small and hard with wildness, / soften and disappear" ("The Givens"). One can grow to like the brief moments of true sweetness ("soft-spoken," which suggests both the furry quality of the branches and their gently threshing movements). But the effect may be too frail to bear all the meditative observation she asks of it, and of us.

More demanding still are the moments of climax and crisis that spill over from the actual ecstasy, never exactly in the center of the lens, onto details of livid relief: "The waiter's hand on the wineglass / seemed an intermediary flame, / the atoms rampant inside it" ("Chanel No. 5"); her lover holds out a seashell and she sees on his finger a freshly stitched cut with a "row of faint commas" and a "wavering white splice" that remind her of "the delicate little seam / dividing the testicles" ("The Cut"); the lover stands at the balcony watching sundown "run over the slow swells," the pleasure boats "shuddering." She stands beside him. They appear not to be looking at one another as "his thumb not quite touched // my nipple, which shriveled, / and with the other hand slowly // unbuttoned and unzipped himself, / all the while watching the pleasure boats // glide past us trailing bits of broken mirror, / their engines pulsing steadily, // fueled by what's left of the future" ("Revenge").

In this domain of inevitable and somewhat mad melancholy, even the titles hint at the effect of swift tearing by small teeth. (Louise Glück's *House on Marshland* often had this feeling of childish rage.) Of course the future is almost used up; of course the couple are so depleted by their Spenglerian mood they no longer gaze upon each another; and, still, of course they are such exemplars of overripe and inexhaustible sexual heat that they can keep summoning themselves to devastating performances of romantic lust. These attitudes unfold in quaintly privileged surroundings like the following: "The hotel's heating system blurts / sporadic clouds into the faint / geometry of unlit monoliths / beyond a flimsy Spanish balcony. / That, of all things, is what I see" ("Worldliness").

It is of interest that the design for the jacket of Twichell's *Perdido* shows an anonymous painting on a sand dollar of four speckled eels, their ferocious, forward-slung lower jaws somewhat stylized and sleekened by the artist. The current fascination with the shark to the contrary notwithstanding, there is surely no creature of the deep more vicious, no predator more removed from empathy. As an emblem of the ideal of passionate self-sacrifice with which this poet, at least hypothetically, attempts to align herself, the eel may also hint at the inhuman remove and brutal dumbness that await the appetites so honed and excited. The outcome is carnage with none of the inspiration (or deftness) of resistance.

Galway Kinnell is an accomplished navigator of the sensory. Having during his poetic career penetrated the various sidechapels of myth worship and the egocentric surreal, Kinnell now "composes" (in the double sense of writing and striking the attractive pose) with no suggestion of effort. Hence many of the poems are genial tableaux of pleasurable perceptual suspense. Even in satiety his *personae* are decorously reserved, which only increases the riveting effect of the sexuality. "The Perch," "Last Gods" (with its atmosphere of uncanny tenderness as the man orally stimulates the woman), and the last poem in the sequence "When One Has Lived a Long Time Alone"—all celebrate the fiery swoon of sex against a background of pantheistic approval. Even the indifferent cosmos blesses the unions so pearled with perfection:

> When one has lived a long time alone,
> one wants to live again among men and women,
> to return to that place where one's ties with the human
> broke, where the disquiet of death and now also

of history glimmers its firelight on faces,
. . . where lovers speak,
on lips blowsy from kissing, that language
the same in each mouth, and like birds at daybreak
blether the song that is both earth's and heaven's,
until the sun has risen, and they stand
in a halo of being made one: kingdom come,
when one has lived a long time alone.
                ("When One Has Lived a Long Time Alone," 11)

One feels in many of the new poems the breath of a trouba-
dour dawn, cold, dewy, erotic, alive with birdsong, in an atmo-
sphere of reverence arresting the alert imagination.

It is equally characteristic that in another poem he should
present himself inclined against the mantel, with the stylized
domestic sophistication one associates with the narrator of *Six
Chapters of a Floating Life*, as he looks into the innocently ob-
scene bloom of an orchid, and that then, almost unwittingly,
he should put on the player a Romantic sonata. More even
than with the field of unmediated sense perception (although
cognate with it), Kinnell is at home with music, its history and
interpretation, and with the habit of listening to music in
many moods. So when after attending a performance of
Haydn's Symphony in F-sharp Minor he imagines the depar-
ture of the musicians into an earlier age after the last adagio,
we believe in the symbolic truth of the details, even if realisti-
cally they are somewhat fanciful in their rusticity:

Before leaving each player blows
the glimmer off the music-stand candle,
where fireweed, dense blazing star, flame azalea stored it sum-
        mers ago,
puffing that quantity of darkness into the hall
and the same portion of light
into the elsewhere where the players reassemble and wait . . .
                                            ("Farewell")

What the musicians await is an oboist in the woods who will
tune their instruments to a perfect A so as to encourage the
creatures and elements in their diurnal cycle, awakening the

birds, but also helping the musicians to "play / the phrases inside flames wobbling on top of stalks in the field . . . and in gnats whining past in a spectral bunch." Even in daylight the knowledge of death eclipses the spirit. So, almost immediately, the dawn slides over into night again, and the elegy for the poet Paul Zweig, who died in 1984 nearing fifty, takes shape in the duet of the violinists who "scathe the final phrases":

> In the darkness above the stage I imagine
> the face of my old friend Paul Zweig
> —who went away, his powers intact, into Eternity's Woods
>     alone, under a double singing of birds—
> . . . . . . . . . . . . . . . . . . . . . . . . . . . . . . . . .
> The bow-hairs still cast dust on the bruised wood.
> Everything on earth, born
> only moments ago, abruptly tips over
> and is dragged by mistake into the chaotic inevitable.
> Goodbye, dear friend.
>
> ("Farewell")

These moments are gripping in their coherence of response. In this poem, as almost everywhere in this book, we never look blurredly through the ambiguousness of perception—the half-glimpsed, the out-of-articulate-reach. Instead, feeling is exact and immediate, apprehended forcefully by the sensibilities and directly spoken by the poetic instrument. Indeed, one can scarcely avoid the metaphor of musical skill when admiring the highly organized array of verbal responses in these poems to the physical responses implied by their themes. Kinnell is very much the adept summoning up and redeploying his experience of audition throughout the altered context of emotional reawakening. The technique of fine recoil from the obvious (including the subtle reference to his own past work) provides frequent pleasure:

> The audience straggles from the hall and at once disappears.
> For myself I go on foot on Seventh Avenue
> down to the little, bent streets of the West Village.

From ahead of me comes the *hic* of somebody drunk
and then the *nunc* of his head bumping against the telephone
    pole.

("Farewell")

Accompanied by an almost comforting rue, the bereaved friend and fellow poet reenters the world of the exigent and drunkenly broken and yet undeniably benevolent here and now.

Unlike Kinnell, the Irish poet Eavan Boland divines in the local reality not the sensual but rather a species of the supernatural; it is a supernatural inflected, however, by the fact that it is embedded in an historical immediacy alien to Americans. Although I realize that she has already been superbly reviewed by Susan Stewart,[1] Boland's poetry is sufficiently striking to me that I wanted to echo and slightly extend Stewart's scrupulous attention to her.

One implication I would bring out from the earlier review's emphasis on the theme of historical entanglement and the tonalities of suffering is the importance of the local. The "local" has much higher resolution, as it were, in the work of Boland than in that of most American poets. It is a terrain crowded and peopled and poignant in almost directly inverse proportion to its current appearance of abandonment and dereliction. The shore where the villagers moved their huts to be closer to the edible seaweed during the famines is now a stretch of empty scree. Or rather, this vacant place of water and grinding stones is alive with the historical significations and losses that act as a collective *genius loci*, haunting and interrogating the people of today under a palimpsest of indistinction.[2]

Some years ago W. H. Auden suggested that what American poets found difficult even to *see* in the work of European poets, because they lacked it in their own culture, was a twin sense—of the long-standing social continuity (even that of class bias) between persons, and of coordination between place and person.

> Until quite recently an English writer, like one of any European country, could presuppose two conditions, a nature which was mythologized, humanized, on the whole friendly, and a human

society which had become in time, whatever succession of invasions it may have suffered in the past, in race and religion more or less homogeneous and in which most people lived and died in the locality where they were born.[3]

Doubtless Auden would want to modify his notion of nature's humanization in light of the inexorably infernal subsequent progress of ecological disaster and nuclear radiation, and equally doubtless Boland herself will feel uncomfortable to have a Briton like Auden cited to shed light on things Irish. Still, I believe his assertions of thirty-five years ago illuminate a major difference between Boland and us: that *her* natural world, still agriculturally precarious, is everywhere imaginatively inhabited, while ours is more likely to be either indefinite, or merely plowed, settled, and paved.

One association sets Boland apart from most American poets, and that is the one between place and speech. Where we might think of the wilderness as pathless and wordless and without record, Boland constantly asserts (as the title of one poem has it): "We are human history, we are not natural history." Even more, she believes that the natural and the human are inextricable. A surf of blossoming hawthorne hedges in the May dusk speak "the only language spoken in these parts." But it is a language of curse and dying and forsakenness. Revolutionary Ireland is "the country of our malediction." In a homely kitchen her grandmother tells her mother as a child the story of "what we lost," which, even as it is told, abrades and thins out in the memory:

> The fields are dark already.
> The frail connections have been made and are broken.
> The dumb-show of legend has become language,
> is becoming silence and who will know that once
>
> words were possibilities and disappointments.
>
> ("What We Lost")

As a rough charm against the disappearance of the clear meaning of the words for the truth, the poet attempts to keep her language, like a wound, raw: "[M]y speech will not heal. I do not want it to heal" ("In Exile").

As one might expect, this poet is diffident of inheritance, arduously discriminating the forebears she will consent to follow and be moved by. Although clearly stirred by gardens and flowers, she resists the appeal of personification almost successfully. In one poem, a friend, who is well enough off to have both a garden and a conservatory for hothouse blooms, tells the poet the story of a local girl who marries a merchant and is taken to sea by him. Boland shies at the suggestion that more can exist in nature than the natural.

> I thought the garden looked so at ease.
> The roses were beginning on one side.
> The laurel hedge was nothing but itself,
> and all of it so free of any need
> for nymphs, goddesses, wounded presences—
> ("Daphne Heard with Horror the Addresses of the God")

For all that, Boland herself is patently yielding to the suggestion of animate sorrow, "the fleet river-daughters who took root / and can be seen in the woods in / unmistakable shapes of weeping." She and the companion who pours their tea are also mentally turning and touching again in the homely anecdote the ageless mystery of money (the merchant) and rapine (the innocent local girl bartered against her future), responding in a subtly womanly way to what Philip Larkin too neatly labeled the "religious wounding" at the wedding night.

"Myth," claims Eavan Boland, "is the wound we leave / in the time we have." To ponder that assertion is to begin to recognize how meager she believes her resources to be, how starved her sensibilities, how unsatisfied by the available retellings of the past. So when, in the poem from which the assertion derives, she reinstalls herself in the role of Ceres gazing hopelessly after Demeter, we also feel the extent to which her shocked recognition of the resemblance is a source of desolation rather than reconciliation with her past. In her case, time is this "March evening / at the foothills of the Dublin Mountains, / across which the lights have changed all day, // holding up my hand / sickle-shaped, to my eyes / to pick out / my own daughter from / all the other children in the distance; // her back turned to me" ("The Making of an Irish Goddess"). If there were a danger of poetry being extinguished altogether and I were allowed only one poem by Eavan Boland to rescue from oblivion, it would be this one. "The Making of an Irish Goddess" contains all the themes dear to her combined with complete transparency, an effect of terrific velocity, and the devotion to an ideal of meaning newly realized in place.

In the work of Pamela Alexander we hear an unusual ventriloquism, speaking for an ethos of work different from that we find in this century. Instead of the labor that drains and dehumanizes, Alexander celebrates the love of one's own excellent skill—"our working joy," as her protagonist puts it. For rather than an imitation of the gross, general, depressed, and demotic voices we overhear in many colloquial contemporaries, Alexander takes on the voice of an idiosyncratic and lively elevation. This elegance, moreover, coheres with a character of quite specific demeanor and vocation—that of the French emigré, naturalist, hunter, taxidermist, tutor, miller, and painter John James Audubon.

The gentle filtration the poet performs on Audubon's creole is one that Robert Penn Warren, for example, did not achieve in his Audubon monologues. The result is more strikingly indigenous than we hear in Warren, who may distract us too far with his insistent archaic drawl. After a time spent reading Alexander's *Commonwealth of Wings*, however, no style at all seems to obtrude on the simple, lively flame of Audubon's rendered voice: "Daily I lose myself & live / as Creature. . . . my body loosens toward the air, which is a greater body, / its brilliant passages limitless / over waves, its dark paths tilting through mangrove branches. / I share it with a commonwealth of wings" ("Air"). In another poem, Audubon writes his wife from his first secure employment in three years, tutoring a spoiled, sickly Southern child named Miss Pirrie in her "rivery murmurous sanctuary" above New Orleans. Her doctor has prescribed total indulgence of her every whim: "For five months the magnolias / have steadied us, five months of sturdy work. / Joseph [Audubon's draftsman-assistant] is able, drafting plants. . . . Only my student / lags, her sketches sullen, her health poxy. . . . She calls / for sugar cakes all afternoon, and I am relieved of educating her artful urges. I take / my freedom quickly to the forest" ("My Ornithology Proceeds"). The doctor's suspicion of Audubon's morals flickers in the lines, though with a little chill seeping downward from the speaker's disinterested repugnance ("her artful urges"). The tone is tactfully and succinctly handled. And when he speaks of his gift for seeing and his tenacity in following the exotic species across the continent, he is clear about what he has achieved, and at what cost:

> I know them, their shapes & movements, their differing atti-
> tudes
> of being still. . . .
> . . . . . . . . . . . . .
>                 I have followed them
> where no other man has gone, have shot
> & ate them, or pierced & posed them on wires for Drawing,
> have named and made them famous.
>
>                                         ("Reprise")

The persona poem or, as here, the persona volume, appeals to many differently talented poets. One of the unlikeliest masters of this sort is Donald Finkel, who no sooner steps off into somebody else's voice than he becomes flexible, magisterial, capable of any effect of madness, lyricism, cleverness, or superstitious awe. Had Finkel taken on the Audubon theme, we would doubtless be reading a very different book of poems, one with stronger grooves and outlines, as if carried into a major from a minor register, or executed in a different aesthetic medium. But even Finkel could not, I think, have bettered the chronic gentle cheerfulness that permeates Alexander's impression of Audubon's character:

> I am a collection of landscapes,
> a Gazetteer. Of griefs & hopes
> & consummations. I must be old now, although
> I think so only in the company of mirrors. I cannot
> summarize myself. Alone,

at American Falls, years ago,
I saw they were motion more
than Substance, wrote *cannot be drawn*
& walked behind into white
translucence . . .

("Sight")

## NOTES

1. Also in *APR*. See Susan Stewart, "After the Ancients and After the Moderns," *APR* ( July/August 1991).

2. See Boland's article "Outside History," which appeared in *APR* in June 1990 along with the twelve poems grouped under the same title, to which I make reference.

3. W. H. Auden, "American Poetry" [1956] in *The Dyer's Hand* (New York: Vintage, 1962).

## UNDER DISCUSSION
### Donald Hall, General Editor

Volumes in the Under Discussion series collect reviews and essays about individual poets. The series is concerned with contemporary American and English poets about whom the consensus has not yet been formed and the final vote has not been taken. Titles in the series include:

Forthcoming volumes will examine the work of Gwendolyn Brooks, Langston Hughes, and Muriel Rukeyser, among others.

*Please write for further information on available editions and current prices.*

**Ann Arbor**          The University of Michigan Press